Up and Down

Sarah Todd Hammer   Jennifer Starzec

Copyright © 2018 by Sarah Todd Hammer and Jennifer Starzec

All rights reserved. No part of this publication may be reproduced, distributed, or transmitted in any form or by any means, including photocopying, recording, or other electronic or mechanical methods, without the prior written permission of the authors, except in the case of brief quotations used in critical reviews and certain other noncommercial uses permitted by copyright law.

Printed in the United States of America

Hammer, Sarah Todd; Starzec, Jennifer

Up and Down/ Sarah Todd Hammer; Jennifer Starzec

Also Written By

Sarah Todd Hammer and Jennifer Starzec:

5k, Ballet, and a Spinal Cord Injury

Determination

*One-third of all proceeds from this book are donated to the Make-A-Wish Foundation. However, sometimes we may donate to different charities for specific events. We reserve the right to do so.

· · ·

This book is about true events. However, some people's names have been changed to protect their identity. Some details may not be exactly as they happened in real life. The events are as the authors remember them.

Content Warning:

The first chapter of Premiere Piano deals with mentions of depression and mental illness. Details are kept very vague, however.

There are also a few mentions of anxiety related to health (due to history of emotional trauma from transverse myelitis) throughout this book.

Of course, there are also many detailed descriptions of hospital settings and medical tests.

We know we have readers with mental illnesses, and though we hope nothing in this book is triggering, we want to ensure that you are all safe!

Dedication

For Harry. There are no words I can say that will ever truly express how thankful I am for you.

- Sarah Todd

For Mackenzie T.

- Jen

In Loving Memory

of

Pauline Siegel.

Without Pauline and her husband, Sandy, there would be no Transverse Myelitis Association.

www.myelitis.org

Table of Contents

Prelude — 11

I. Premiere Piano — 15

II. Key Change — 79

III. Final Forte — 135

Afterword — 183

Finale — 185

Acknowledgments — 191

Prelude

Without music, what would life be?

During times of crisis, during times of despair, rhythms and notes have always been there.

It's easy to get caught up in all life throws, but a few sweet lyrics can save our spirits.

Up and Down

Premiere Piano

"'Cause nobody saves me, baby, the way you do"

- One Direction, "Fireproof"

Sarah Todd

Everyone deserves to have something or someone in their life that makes them happy. And at ten years old, I'd already found mine.

I'd been begging my mom to help me apply for a Wish to be granted by the Make-A-Wish Foundation for awhile. She'd told me that early on, she'd visited their website and had determined that I would most likely not be eligible for a Wish, but as I saw other children with TM receiving Wishes, I was pretty confident that I would qualify.

It's not easy trying to be happy all the time. Although I make it look easy, it isn't always. Once I discovered One Direction, I slowly began to rely on them to make me happy. I was only ten years old and didn't understand why I was so unhappy or how *unhealthy* my unhappiness was. I felt like I was a happy girl, but then I'd experience dark thoughts when I was lying in bed at night thinking or sitting in class at school, dealing with intrusive thoughts when I should've been learning.

Fourth grade. I was only in *fourth grade*. And Harry Styles was the person who was keeping me going. I couldn't explain it, but he just was.

Up and Down

Just like it's not easy trying to be happy all the time, it's not easy living with a disability—especially as a child. I think that's what brought my depression on: my loss of normalcy. My life as a ten-year-old wasn't how I thought it would be. I didn't particularly enjoy having a paraprofessional follow me around at school all day or getting asked weird, personal questions about my body and health no ten-year-old should get asked or going to a never-ending stream of therapy and doctor appointments. It made sense that I was unhappy; I was dealing with a life-altering situation. But now, six years later, I'm as happy as can be, and that happiness is real.

And I can only credit one person.

. . . .

"Should I wear this shirt or this shirt?" I asked my mom, debating between the two.

"Definitely that one," my mom said, pointing to the One Direction shirt. "It goes really well with your skirt." She was right. It did. So I chose that shirt, and she helped me put it on.

"I'm so excited!" I told her as I hopped in the passenger seat of her car, ready to head to Chick-Fil-A to meet my grandmother for a lunch date. It was one of our favorite places to eat together.

My mom stilled. "Why?" she asked, seemingly nervous.

"I'm sitting in the front seat!" I exclaimed, excited that this was my first time getting shotgun. I was twelve and *finally* tall enough to sit in the front. It was a big deal!

"Oh," she said, looking much more relaxed. I wondered why, but I didn't say anything.

On the ride to Chick-Fil-A, I looked up where One Direction was going to be performing next, always eager to keep up with what they were doing. "They'll be in Detroit next," I told Mom. "They're doing two shows there! One on the sixteenth and one on the seventeenth." If only they could play two shows in Atlanta...

When we pulled into a parking space, I hopped out of the car with my mom, excited to see my grandma. When I got to the doors of the restaurant, my mom opened them for me, and we went inside, where we were greeted by a worker. "Hi! I love your shirt!" she told me enthusiastically, and I thanked her with a smile. I expected to head to the counter to order or find my grandma at a table, but the woman spoke again. "Do you want to follow me over here? Let's head to the back!" I was confused, but I followed the woman anyway, curious. There was a room in the back of the restaurant that I guessed she was leading me to, and I could see five shadows through the window. I knew something fishy was going on, but I couldn't place my finger on it until we were right outside the door to the room.

I had a feeling I knew what was going on.

Oh my god, I thought apprehensively, *Is that One Direction in there?* It was a naive thought, but there *were* five shadows, and the woman *had* complimented my One Direction shirt. I didn't have much time to think about it, because she opened the door, and I was greeted by five girls in Make-A-Wish Georgia shirts, all with huge smiles on their faces. "Your Wish is coming true!" they yelled excitedly, nearly making my heart stop. I sat down on the chair right by the door and put my hand over my mouth, shocked.

It was then that I heard the One Direction music blasting and saw the One Direction decorations, pictures, and gifts around the room, and I knew which Wish of mine was being granted: the only one I truly wanted. "You need to pack your bags *tonight*, because tomorrow, you're flying to Detroit to meet One Direction!" one of my Wish granters exclaimed.

"Oh my god!" I cried. Tears immediately spilled down my face; I was *so* happy. "Thank you!" I told my Wish granters and proceeded to give them all hugs. There truly were no words I could say to express how happy I was in that moment. It was one of those moments where there really is *nothing* to say. I was going to get to hug and talk to the very people who'd helped me through my hardest times. It didn't feel real. I was overwhelmed. This was *actually* happening, and to *me*!

We sat down and ate chicken nuggets and ice cream while we listened to One Direction music and I opened gifts. One of my Wish granters handed me a picture of One Direction with a picture of me photoshopped in and said, "You won't need this in a couple days; you'll have the real thing!" And that made me even *more* excited, if that were even possible.

At home after my surreal Wish reveal, I danced around in my Make-A-Wish Georgia shirt they gave me, incredibly excited. My whole body felt warm, the excitement building up within me, and I just couldn't wait to be with my favorite band. I got to surprise my best friend, too, because she and her mom were coming with us, and she couldn't believe it. "Really?" she kept saying over and over. I felt the same way!

The next morning, the four of us drove to the airport, all wearing our Make-A-Wish Georgia t-shirts. My best friend and I had so much energy; we didn't stop smiling. As we were going through security, one of the TSA agents asked us, "Are you going somewhere fun?"

"Yes!" we all replied, huge grins on our faces.

"Disney World?" he asked, of course assuming we were going to the place where most Wishes occurred.

"No! We're going to meet One Direction!" I told him, not even really believing the words I'd just said.

I kept thinking that everyone at our gate was probably wondering why we were going to Detroit for a Make-A-Wish trip, but little did they know what we were going to get to do! The hotel Make-A-Wish put us in was extremely nice, and I found myself loving Detroit despite the preconceptions I had of the city. We hung-out at the pool there once we arrived, and then we went out for dinner.

All throughout our meal, my best friend and I kept getting engaged in the conversation, but then we'd remember that we were going to hug and talk to our favorite people in the entire world the next day. "It just hit me!" we kept saying randomly, letting out deep breaths. The anticipation was crazy. I'd never been so excited for anything before.

The next day, the day of my Wish, we basically spent the *entire* day getting ready. We bought a cute black and green striped dress for me to wear to meet the boys, and then we ordered room service, painted our nails, and did our hair and makeup. I was extremely excited, but also slightly nervous, so I had trouble eating because of the apprehension. This was my one chance to spend time with the people who'd changed my life, so I needed to take advantage of it.

My friend's mom painted my nails black and wrote "1D" for One Direction on my big toes and thumbs, and my mom gave me a bracelet that said "Directioner" on it to wear along with my Harry necklace. We did my hair in one long side braid with a black, sparkly headband, and I put on a little bit of makeup. One of the main things I wanted to do when I met the boys was give them mine and Jen's book, *5k, Ballet, and a Spinal Cord Injury*, so I wrote a note in it and signed it so I could give it to them. I took a picture of what I wrote, and I've never let anyone read it before.

A limo picked us up and took us to Ford Field Stadium, which was *so* cool! Fans outside the arena stared at us, thinking we were One Direction. It was *hilarious*. I felt like a celebrity! We met our Make-A-Wish representative outside the arena, and she took us inside, where we got our tickets (which were on the floor and *very* close to the main stage!) and purchased t-shirts and a program. We watched some of the opening band before Sally, One Direction's assistant tour manager, met us and took us backstage! Tons of fans stared at us (once again!) as the security guards opened the gates and let us back, making me feel incredibly important. Sally, who had an adorable British accent, walked us outside the room where we were going to meet them and talked to us while we waited. My mom showed Sally my book and told her I wanted to give it to the boys, and she was very impressed. At one point, I saw Louis walking away from us down the hall, and I turned to my friend and exclaimed, "There's Louis!" It was so crazy that we were going to be hugging him and talking to him so soon!

We ended up having to wait quite a while, even once we were allowed in the room. Sally said the boys were eating dinner when we asked where they were, which made me laugh. But when they finally came in the room, Niall and Liam walked in first, followed by Louis and Zayn, and then Harry, my *favorite*, came in last. I was standing quite close to the doorway, so when Harry came in, he turned towards me, squatted slightly, waved, and said, "Hi!" with a smile. I was so much shorter than he was; I was only 4'10", while he was 6'1"!

When I finally got to go meet the boys, our Wish representative told them my name, and I hesitated for a second as I saw all the boys looking at me. Niall motioned me over with a smile and gave me a big hug while rubbing my back, and all the others greeted me with kind smiles and hugs, too. Harry was the last one I hugged, and after I did, I told them all about the book, and I handed it to Harry since he was on the end.

"Amazing!" Harry interrupted me after I'd just said that I wrote the book, making me blush.

"You wrote that?! That's the book?!" Niall asked while Harry flipped through the pages, and I smiled and nodded. Harry made the most enthusiastic face while looking through the book, making me smile so wide. Thankfully, the Wish representative snapped a photo of us at the perfect time! All the boys gathered around to look at the book, all clearly impressed, making me so happy. They were some of the most famous people in the world, yet they cared about me and what I'd accomplished. I felt like the most special girl ever. We posed for a picture, and I stood on the end until Harry nudged me and told me to get in the middle. "I'm gonna hold the book," he said, a proud expression on his face. He truly loves making people happy, and he knew he was doing just that. In our picture, he posed with the book open and made an enthusiastic face yet again as he bent down closer to my height, making for an adorable photo. After we took the picture, I looked up at his smiling face and leaned in for another hug. He was so warm and sweet; the feeling I got when hugging him is indescribable. I told him I loved him before I chickened out as I pulled away, and he smiled sweetly and said, "I love you more!"

And those four words changed me so much.

The boys proceeded to sign my t-shirt for me, and Mom got a few more pictures of them while they did. I was so sad to watch them leave the room, but they were incredibly polite and told us to enjoy the show. My best friend and I hugged and cried tears of joy as we walked back to the crowd, and the same fans who stared at us when we walked backstage stared at us again. I couldn't believe what had just happened; it was so surreal.

And it got even better.

During the concert, Harry was somehow able to find me in the crowd! He bent down a little bit and waved frantically, smiling widely. I waved back, and he smiled again before continuing to dance and sing like the fabulous performer he is. I was so sad that I was done meeting the boys, but the concert was incredible, too, and so was the rest of our vacation! We swam at the pool the next day and looked at all our pictures, admittedly crying both out of sadness the experience was over and happiness that it'd happened.

About a month later, Make-A-Wish put together a thank you book for the boys full of pictures from Wishes they'd granted because they'd granted so many, and I got to write a letter to put in the book! I hand wrote a three page letter to the boys, and it was put on the very first page along with pictures I sent in! I've never let anyone except my mom read the letter, as it was extremely personal to me, and I never will.

Up and Down

I have such a special relationship with the boys, especially Harry, and I love being able to share that with them. I'll cherish them and what they've done for me for the rest of my life.

"Sun is up and the color's blinding. Take the world and redefine it"

- The Greatest Showman, "Come Alive"

Jen

I looked out the window of the train, watching the houses and trees turn into tall buildings as we went from suburbs to city. I sighed audibly, turning back to face my mom, who was sitting on the worn, brown seat in front of me.

"So, what doctor am I seeing today, again?" I questioned, clearly a little annoyed with having to go to yet another appointment.

"Neurologist."

"Didn't I *just* see my neuro?"

My mom just shrugged. I crossed my arms and sat back, feeling the ugly, plastic-y material of the train seat stick to and rub against my skin.

"Aren't you at least glad that you get to miss school today? You get a long weekend," Mom asked me after a short moment of silence.

"I'd rather go to school," I mumbled only semi-coherently.

"What?"

"Never mind."

I turned back to face the window, taking in the familiar sights of the city and realizing at once how nice a day it was outside. It was the Friday of Labor Day weekend, which is arguably one of the nicest times of the year in

Chicago, and the sky was bright blue. I didn't see one cloud up there, and earlier, I'd noticed that it was pleasantly warm and hardly windy. It was a perfect morning, which I really wished I could spend outside instead of trapped in that chilly, antiseptic-scented hospital. I couldn't wait to get that appointment over with.

Suddenly, my window went dark, which I knew meant that we had arrived at Union Station. As the train stopped, my mom and I made our way to the doors.

"*Caution. The doors are about to close,*" the automated voice said behind us as we exited the train and began making our way through the station.

"Hm, that's weird," I heard my mom say suddenly.

"What?" I asked, turning to see her looking down at her phone.

"They had to move your appointment back an hour or so."

I groaned. So much for getting it over with.

"No, this is okay, though! This just means we can go to breakfast before the appointment," Mom assured me. "How about Wildberry?"

I perked up a little at this. I was always up for eating at Wildberry Café.

So, my mom and I exited the station and began the walk to the restaurant, which was near Millenium Park, just a little over a mile away from where we were at Union Station. My mom led the way while I kept myself occupied by looking around at the bustling city, completely lost in my thoughts.

As we neared Wildberry, something caught my eye. Or, rather, some*one*. A few yards away, walking towards us, was a lady who looked *exactly* like Sarah Todd's mom.

The sea of people around the lady thinned slightly, revealing a familiar-looking little blonde girl walking next to her, which made me do a double-take.

"Wait, what? Sarah Todd?" I squealed, running towards the pair and hugging my friend. Our moms laughed, clearly proud of themselves for pulling off the surprise.

"Do I still have an appointment, then?" I asked my mom, still a little confused. She shook her head.

"Nope. The day is free!"

As the four of us walked into Wildberry together, I grinned widely, happy that this day that I envisioned as being so horribly boring was turning around completely.

• • • •

After we were all incredibly full from breakfast, Sarah Todd's mom wanted to do as many touristy things as possible, and I found that our day had pretty much been planned out already. After stopping by Sarah Todd's hotel for a little bit, we headed over to the first tourist attraction that her mom wanted to do: an architecture boat tour.

We boarded the boat, which was fairly large but quite simple in appearance. At the top, there were many rows of white seats, which was where we were supposed to sit during the tour. Underneath the deck with the seats was a wall of windows all the way around. I couldn't see what was behind them, as they were darkened, but I assumed there was some sort of room under the deck. In front of that, there was another open deck forming the pointed front of the boat, and painted on the side was "Chicago's Leading Lady."

We sat down in the white, plastic seats near the front, not far from where the tour guide was standing. After everyone else had gotten on and found seats, the man started talking and the boat slowly began to move. As the boat made its way through the Chicago River, the man pointed out and explained a lot of the buildings and structures we passed. Chicago has a lot of unique architecture, and though I was already familiar with the majority of the buildings he pointed out, I was learning some new things about my city. I looked over at the others, and Sarah Todd's mom seemed to be very interested in everything the tour guide was saying. It was nice to see her having such a great time.

However, it was getting very hot. The boat was completely open with no shade to be seen, and the sun beat down on us hard. I felt my confused nerves fire up and begin to make my skin feel like it was on fire.

Sarah Todd seemed to be feeling similarly. I looked over and her face was flushed, and she looked very uncomfortable. She also looked incredibly bored.

"I'm so hot. We should seek shade," Sarah Todd said, as if reading my mind. I nodded in agreement and we looked around, then noticed a spot where stairs led to the lower level. After informing her mom about where we were headed, we went down the stairs, where we found ourselves in a fairly large room, empty of people but filled with little tables and chairs.

Cool air hit us immediately, which felt incredible. We passed what I assumed was a small bar and sat at one of the tables right in front of one of many windows overlooking the river.

We simply talked for awhile, catching up on things that had happened in our lives since we'd last seen each other, like Sarah Todd's Make-A-Wish trip and the start of school. Once conversation dwindled, we took out our phones and looked through our apps for something to entertain us. We found a face-swapping app, and decided to face-swap a bunch of random pictures, each result as funny as the rest.

"I LOOK SO WEIRD!" Sarah Todd exclaimed, cracking up, after we swapped her and Harry Styles' faces. It was just a silly little thing, but for whatever reason, we could not stop laughing. I could already tell it was going to be a great weekend.

Up and Down

"I want you here with me, like how I pictured it, so I don't have to keep imagining"

- One Direction, "Something Great"

Sarah Todd

I'd never been to Chicago before, and it felt incredibly strange being so close to Jen without her knowing. I sat in my hotel room, giddy, and texted her with a huge grin on my face. As I texted her, I had to be extremely careful, especially when I sent her a screenshot of something—I didn't want her to notice my phone was on Central Time instead of Eastern! She had no idea I was only an hour away from her, which I felt slightly bad about, but I knew she would be excited when I surprised her the next day. The plan was to meet up with her and her mom at Wildberry for breakfast the next morning, and my mom and I would already be waiting in a booth when they walked in. However, as my mom and I made our way across the busy streets of Chicago to Wildberry, we ended up spotting Jen and her mom heading the same way.

I could tell that Jen noticed me after a few seconds, and I gave her a huge smile as her face contorted in confusion before she caught on. "Wait, what?!" she exclaimed as she ran up and gave me a big hug, obviously ecstatic. We immediately took selfies together to share on Instagram, so excited to be reunited with each other. Jen asked how we coordinated the trip, and our moms told her that they'd planned it several months ago and that my mom surprised me with the trip a few days before.

We headed into Wildberry, which was extremely crowded, and asked for a table. We were told that we'd have to wait, so we chatted and caught up with each other outside. Once we were seated, we looked through the menu and ordered some delicious sounding food, and I ended up falling in love with Wildberry. Their pancakes were the best I'd ever had, and I was so disappointed to find that there were only three locations in Illinois and nowhere else, so we made it a point to go back before I had to go home.

Our trip to Chicago was already going amazingly well, and I'd only been with Jen for an hour! Things only seemed to get even more fun, too. For the rest of the day, we ventured around the city, trying to see as many iconic, touristy sights as possible while we were visiting. Of course, that meant we visited The Bean (or "Cloudgate," as I learned it's actually called) in Millenium Park, where we also visited Crown Fountain, an area of art that featured huge screens with faces on them and a fountain. I thought the faces were pretty cool and hilarious, so Jen and I made sure to take a lot of pictures in front of those!

One of the coolest parts about our trip to Chicago was that I got to see 1D in concert twice! It had only been about two weeks since I'd met them, and I wondered if Harry would point me out in the crowd again like he had in Detroit. The first night, our seats were extremely close to the boys, as my mom and I were right next to the mini stage that connected to the catwalk. I wore a shirt we had made with my picture of me with the boys on it, and I was so excited to be seeing my favorite people once again.

I thought it was incredible that Harry was able to point me out in the crowd in Detroit right after I met him, because there were about 50,000 other fans in the crowd that night. Since two weeks had passed, I really didn't think that anything like that would happen, but I hoped it would! And of course, the boys followed through. Because I was so close to them, I could tell they were staring at me every now and then, most likely trying to figure out if it was me. They waved at me a lot, too, but the funniest interaction was with Harry.

My mom was dancing to the music and having a great time (because *of course* she loves 1D, too!), and Harry noticed the both of us. He waved at me a few times, but when he caught sight of my mom being all crazy, he cracked up, causing him to trip on a light close to the edge of the stage and nearly fall. It was so funny, but also simply incredible that he remembered me. All the boys had met so many other Wish kids in the past two weeks and performed in many other cities, but they hadn't forgotten me.

It was impossible not to feel special.

The second night, Jen was being dragged along to the concert with her friends, so that's why my mom decided to buy us tickets, too. We were sitting on the second level, so the boys couldn't see me, but it was still so fun. I was excited that Jen was getting to see 1D in person, too, but she wasn't that interested. She even brought *earplugs*! I thought she was crazy, but she was a good sport about it. Plus, she told me that she loved and respected 1D for how kind they were to me, so I knew she was developing a soft spot for them!

• • • •

Whenever Jen and I see each other, it's always difficult saying goodbye. Most of the time, we don't know when we'll see each other again, and the unknown makes things even harder. I didn't want the car that would take me and my mom to the airport to show up, because I could have easily stayed in Chicago with Jen forever! But of course, it did, and I looked at Jen sadly before squeezing her as tightly as I could in a hug. I got teary like I always do when we say goodbye to each other, and I had to force myself to step away from my sister and hop in the car. I would see her soon—I just didn't know when.

"Rain will make the flowers grow"

- *Les Miserables*, "A Little Fall of Rain"

Jen

"What about this one?" My mom's best friend, Cathy, asked, holding up a gorgeous, ocean-blue dress for me to see. We were in the crowded dress aisle of a store in the mall with her daughter—my friend, Sophia—and my mom, trying to find the perfect Homecoming dresses.

"Oh, I love it!" I exclaimed, reaching my left hand over to rub the fabric between my fingers. She added it to the growing pile of dresses she was holding for me, which I planned on trying on.

The Homecoming dance was one of my favorite times of the year in high school. It feels so stereotypically "girly" to say that, but I actually did enjoy spending hours at the mall shopping for the perfect dress and getting all dressed up for the night, complete with a coordinating manicure, full makeup, and a pretty hair-do, before getting a boatload of pictures taken with my friends. It all made me feel so fancy and pretty, which definitely boosted my self-confidence, if only for the night. I always felt like a "normal" teenager for a little while on those nights, and though I was always incredibly exhausted the next day, it was worth it to me.

This year, my Junior year, was no exception. I was excited for my upcoming third Homecoming dance as the three of us searched through every possible store in the mall for dresses for me and Sophia.

"Oh my gosh, Jen, look at this one!" Sophia exclaimed. I turned around from the dress I was looking at to see her pointing to one of the weirdest dresses I had ever seen. It was stick-straight, like a gigantic leg-warmer, and made of some thick, multi-colored material.

"We should try it on, just for fun," I giggled, very curious to know what it'd look like on a human being. Sophia agreed, so we lifted two of the dresses off the rack and brought them into the dressing room.

I noticed the material was oddly heavy, but when I put it on, it was actually surprisingly comfortable. It fit snugly, but still basically looked like an oversized leg warmer on my body.

Sophia and I had a good laugh over how we looked in those dresses, and her mom took pictures of us in silly poses. But that store proved to have nothing of serious interest, so after we changed back into our normal clothes, we went on to the next store.

As we headed over to Windsor, I started to notice that my left leg felt a little heavy. I couldn't move it normally, so it was dragging and feeling increasingly fatigued the more we walked.

But I was just tired, I reminded myself. We'd been walking around the mall for a couple hours; it wasn't uncommon for my body to get exhausted more quickly than most people, thanks to TM. Plus, I was just getting over a bout of strep throat from the previous week, and it also wasn't unlike my body to have a flare in TM symptoms due to a sickness.

Being terrified of getting TM again was something I knew almost everyone with this disorder—and similar—could relate to, but I pushed that "relapse-anxiety" down and distracted myself by thinking of the task at hand, of finding the perfect dress, which I hoped would be at Windsor.

We walked into the small store and were surrounded by sparkly, colorful Homecoming dresses, and I immediately spotted a gorgeous purple one up on the far wall across from the entrance, which was just what I was looking for.

I pointed it out to my mom, Cathy, and Sophia, then tried rushing over, but my leg was way too tired and heavy for any sort of speed-walking.

I must really be over-doing it today, I thought, but luckily, I'd found a more than suitable dress, so I was able to get home and rest soon enough.

The leg heaviness improved considerably after a good night's sleep, but a little bit of it was still subtly there. And then, the week before the dance, I started coming on with one of those lingering respiratory viruses, much to my annoyance.

I'd *just* gotten over strep the previous week, and now I had a sore throat again, plus a cough and no voice. Luckily, I was feeling well enough to attend the dance by the time it came around, though.

It was even more exhausting than dances usually were, and once again my legs quickly became fatigued. But, since I'd just gotten over both strep and that virus, it seemed understandable; illnesses make everyone a little tired for a while! And anyway, I still had fun, even if I had to take a few more breaks than usual.

• • • •

A week or so after the dance, I sat in the grassy park across from my high school, getting ready for our Home Cross Country meet. Though I thought our course was incredibly boring and loved experiencing new areas when racing at other schools, I enjoyed Home meets. It was nice to not have to take a bus to and from the meet, and it often meant that more of my family and even friends were able to attend and watch me run.

My cough was pretty much gone by now, and my legs felt normal again, to me. I was glad I was over that whole thing and couldn't wait to run in our first Home meet of the season, especially since this late-September afternoon happened to be perfect running weather.

"C'mon, guys! We're warming up," one of my teammates, a senior, shouted to the group of us sitting on that part of the field. I finished tightening the laces on my shoes and made my way over to where girls on my team were gathering to begin our warm-up run.

We began the slow lap around the park, some runners naturally falling more ahead or behind each other depending on individual pace. I started in the middle, at the pace I usually warmed up with, but I immediately found it difficult to keep up.

It had been awhile since I'd last run for real, though, since I'd missed a few practices when I was sick. So, I slowed down, trailing closely behind the end of the group in an attempt to conserve my energy for the actual race. I knew the race was probably going to be a little slower for me than usual, but I hoped my pace would be at least a little faster than it was during this warm-up.

"Good luck, girls!" Coach said, passing by us as we slowed down to a walk after completing the lap.

"Thanks!" we responded, waving. Our group scattered as we headed back to our stuff so we could finish our last-minute preparations for the race: final swigs of Gatorade, sips of water, changing into our uniforms, lacing up our spikes.

The first whistle sounded, signaling for all the girls in this race to make their way over to the starting line, where I did my last-minute stretches, trying to stretch out the dull ache that had begun growing in my legs.

"On your marks!"

Everyone got into position, completely still and silent.

The shrill of the final whistle filled the air, and the whole line of girls was off.

Immediately, though, something felt off. After the first couple yards, my pace gradually slowed. My legs felt like huge bricks, and with each step they felt heavier and heavier. One by one, every single runner in the race passed me as I got slower and slower.

My left leg began dragging much like it had in the mall a couple weeks before, but even worse. Then, my knees started buckling and muscles tightening to where I couldn't straighten my legs all the way, so I was "running" with bent legs, further slowing my pace. By now, though, I couldn't even see the second-to-last runner; everyone was long gone.

I avoided the gaze of everyone on the sidelines as I passed, attempting to put all of my focus on getting to the finish line so I could get the rest of this "race" over with. As I fell farther and farther behind with an almost laughable distance between me and the other runners, I felt increasingly embarrassed. I could just feel everyone's eyes on me.

The short three miles felt longer than a marathon, but finally, the finish line was right in front of me, where my concerned coach, mom, and teammates were gathered. As soon as my feet touched the spray-painted white line, I collapsed onto the grass.

• • • •

Technically, we usually weren't allowed to leave Cross Country meets before they were over, but naturally, my coach made an exception. A couple of my friends and my mom helped me walk over to her car, and we left almost immediately.

"Well, it was probably dumb of me to run so soon after being sick. It was just a little overexertion. We know that can cause a little more weakness and stuff sometimes," I said to my mom during the car ride home.

She nodded. "I guess you just have to rest for a little bit."

So, I did. I rested the remainder of that night, and by morning, besides a little bit of achiness in my legs, I felt pretty normal.

I went to school as usual, and the pain in my legs gradually grew throughout the day, but it was fine. It was Fall, after all, which meant lots of fluctuating weather changes that often made my neuropathic pain a little worse. It wasn't anything horrible, and for the most part I felt as though the morning was a pretty normal one.

After lunch, I had choir. After warming up for the first few minutes of class, my choir director, Mrs. White, had us stand up to rehearse one of our songs.

"Jen, you're wobbling. You should sit down," my friend, Angela, whispered to me after we finished going through the first song. I noticed that my legs felt a tad tired, and they still hurt a little bit, but I didn't feel that unsteady.

I shrugged. "I'm fine, Ang. I can stand."

She gave me a look but didn't have a chance to press it, as we needed to get our sheet music out for the next song.

••••

My legs continued to feel a little tired the rest of the day, especially my left leg, but not bad like at the mall the week before or at the cross country meet. The pain continued to worsen, though, and by that evening it was pretty distracting. I laid a heating pad over them and absentmindedly massaged the most painful spots as I did my homework.

When I woke up the next morning, as I tried to stand up from bed, my legs buckled and gave out from beneath me.

"There's a million things I haven't done. Just you wait, just you wait"

- *Hamilton,* "Alexander Hamilton"

Sarah Todd

I'd been to Baltimore too many times to count, with all of those trips being specifically for medical appointments and tests. It seemed like all the air travel I ever did was for medical stuff, either to Kennedy Krieger Institute (KKI), the Mayo Clinic, or Shriners Hospital, aside from my Make-A-Wish and our latest trip to Chicago. Sometimes, I'd dread my upcoming trip to Baltimore for a month before we even left, just because I knew there were so many unpleasantries lying ahead of me. I'd yet to experience flying to Baltimore for fun, and I so desperately wanted to know what it felt like to board a plane to Baltimore and not have anything to dread once I landed. My mom did always incorporate fun activities into our medical trips, and I was slowly warming up to Baltimore (it was like my second home!), but I still hated the feeling of worrying about my painful tests and long, boring appointments beforehand.

When I was last in Baltimore, while I was doing therapy in the gym, we overheard other patients discussing the Baltimore Running Festival. Apparently, Kennedy Krieger had their own team, and every year, patients had the opportunity to participate. I learned that patients who couldn't move their legs walked the 5k with the help of their therapists, and other patients completed the race with arm cycles. Always a ballerina at heart, I never imagined myself participating in a race, especially when it was difficult for me to run. My arms always flopped around when I attempted to run, and I was slightly self-conscious of that after a girl in my class informed me I "look like a deer" when I run. But Mom told me I didn't have to run the 5k, that I could walk, which got me fully onboard.

My physical therapist was the one in charge of KKI's team for the city's festival, and she talked up how exciting the event was and convinced Mom and me to participate. Jen knew how 5k races were supposed to go down, and I certainly didn't, but I was looking forward to trying something new. I knew she would think it was super cool that I was taking part in her favorite hobby, just as I thought it was super fun to teach her how to dance.

· · · ·

For the first time ever, in October 2014, my mom and I made a trip to Baltimore that did *not* have any medical related events in the itinerary! As I looked out the plane's window when we were landing, my heart raced eagerly in my chest, a memory coming to mind. Just four years prior, I had boarded my very first flight to Baltimore. And there I was, four years later, flying to Baltimore on the exact same day, but with excitement rather than fear. This time, I wasn't worried about how high the plane would go or how scary it would be when we landed, and I certainly wasn't thinking about two weeks worth of medical appointments. I felt incredibly relieved, so glad I wasn't in nine-year-old Sarah Todd's place, but thirteen-year-old Sarah Todd's place instead.

We stayed at a different hotel this trip, one that was closer to where the festival was taking place. It almost felt like I wasn't even in Baltimore; downtown Baltimore looked like a completely different place than where we normally stayed. The city was full of excitement, all the participants arriving and preparing for the race. My grandparents came in from Virginia, ready to support me and Mom as we did our first 5k together. It was fun being adventurous and trying new things. Baltimore withheld numerous opportunities for me, and I found that I accomplished something every time I visited.

The night before the festival, KKI's team hosted a party, all the team members welcome to attend. That night was one of the first times I felt like a celebrity—I had the opportunity to sign and sell books, and some of the younger kids wanted pictures with me. I was even on the news! The newscaster asked me about Transverse Myelitis and how it affected me, and I was so happy to bring some much needed awareness to my disorder. It was exceptionally neat to see myself on the news that night! I'd gotten a wonderful start to this new adventure.

• • • •

The morning of the run, tons of runners were gathered around downtown, hydrating and warming up. It was a chilly morning, so I was wearing a jacket, and I shivered as we waited for the run to start. But I knew that once the race began I would warm up, anticipating the burn my legs would feel once I crossed the finish line. There were hundreds of cyclists lined up at the starting line, getting ready to race. I was excited to see how their bikes worked, finding it incredible that their arms were strong enough to cycle their way through the whole race. One girl I knew from KKI who also has TM was there, too. Her smile was contagious; I could tell she was excited to be there. Because her legs were paralyzed, she planned to walk the 5k with the help of her leg braces, crutches, and therapists, and I was looking forward to watching her accomplish her goal.

When I began the race, I started walking quickly, wanting to see how fast I could truly finish the 5k. But Mom told me to slow my pace, because she didn't want me to lose my energy after only a few minutes. I listened to her and paced myself, taking in the scenery around us as we walked. There were patrons cheering the participants on at different points, holding up signs and encouraging us to keep going. I smiled and waved at them, their encouragement making me feel extremely proud of myself. Towards the end of the route, I spotted my grandparents, who were waving and cheering Mom and me on. They reminded me that I was almost to the finish line, making me instantly pick up speed.

Four years before, I never would've thought that I'd successfully walk a 5k and receive a medal. I was full of pride when I stepped foot across the finish line, everyone cheering me on. One of my physical therapists picked me up and posed for a celebratory picture with me, carrying on our tradition of our photos together where I'm in her arms. When I received my medal, I eagerly held it up for a picture, feeling so accomplished.

I'd walked a 5k with a spinal cord injury.

Four years ago, I came to KKI for the first time, unaware of how many times I would return and the special connections I would develop with the staff and the city. Baltimore had become a city full of accomplishments and hope for me, ones I look forward to every time I return.

Up and Down

"When your legs don't work like they used to before"

- Ed Sheeran, "Thinking Out Loud"

Jen

"If a completely healthy 16-year-old came in here unable to walk, of course we'd send her straight to the ER. But, your history of this neurological disorder complicates things... It might just be a flare-up that goes back to normal in a few days with some rest," the doctor at the Urgent Care center said to us later that day. She told us to go to the ER if it didn't get better after a day or two.

Because my symptoms can fluctuate so much just from things like weather changes and overexertion (which isn't uncommon for people with TM), I tried not to be too worried, though that proved to be difficult.

Regardless, I really did not want to go to the ER, so I agreed to rest.

But, I stayed home from school and just rested for a couple days, and nothing changed. So, much to my annoyance, it looked like I was going to have to go to the hospital after all.

Since my doctor had called them ahead of time, they brought me back as soon as I got to the ER; I didn't have to sit in the crowded waiting room at all. That still didn't mean I didn't have to wait at all for anything, though. For hours, I got to lie down on the uncomfortable gurney in one of the small Emergency Department rooms that's closed off by a single curtain.

They took blood right away, as usual, and at first they said they would try to get an MRI that night. I hoped that would happen and I hoped there was a chance I wouldn't have to stay overnight, but as it became dark outside and it grew late with still no MRI, they decided to just admit me and do it the next day.

I had very mixed emotions about this. On one hand, I really didn't want to be admitted again; I didn't want this to turn into some extended hospital stay, as I didn't want to miss anymore school. On the other hand, though, I was kind of glad that I didn't have to do the MRI that night, because doing it the next day meant I could mentally prepare myself. Plus, having that time to prepare meant that they'd more likely be able to sedate me for that full brain and spine MRI, which I knew from previous experience would take hours. It's incredibly difficult to lie still in an enclosed machine for such a long period of time, especially after having a couple not-great experiences with it in the past. Having neuropathic pain that's easily exasperated when lying in one position on a hard, plastic bed for hours also makes those long MRIs difficult to go through awake.

Still, though, I wished they could just do that outpatient while I stayed home.

They wheeled me up to my room, which was super tiny, but I was grateful that it was a single room. At least I wouldn't have to worry about a roommate;

I was 16 years old, but on a pediatrics floor where most patients were younger children.

I settled into my classic uncomfortable hospital bed, wishing I was home in my own bed, but I was exhausted enough to fall asleep pretty quickly.

Not only did they do the MRI the next day, as expected, but they also did a spinal tap (also known as a lumbar puncture). I was really worried about getting another spinal tap, remembering the horrible experience I had with my first one in 2011. But, luckily, they made a plan to do the spinal tap right after the MRI and sedate me for everything.

As usual, I opted for the sedative to be given through IV, which I already had in my arm. In no time, the doctor's faces became blurry and their voices sounded far away, and before I knew it, I was asleep.

They had to lighten the sedative very briefly when first sticking the long needle into my lower back for the spinal tap, so I could be awake to tell them if they somehow accidentally stuck it in the wrong spot. I was still way too out of it to care, though; through the thick fog, I faintly felt a pinch in my back, but my body seemed too far away for it to actually hurt. Less than a second later, I was asleep once again.

• • • •

As awful as my first spinal tap had been, at least it was over right away. In the technical sense, that was still true this time, but it left its mark in a really annoying way: a cerebrospinal fluid leak.

Cerebrospinal fluid, or CSF, is the protective fluid that surrounds your brain and spinal cord. The outermost layer of the membranes that cover cerebrospinal fluid is called the dura; if there's a hole in the dura, the fluid can leak out. This isn't uncommon after things like spinal taps, which makes sense considering the needle goes in there to extract some of this fluid for testing.

Since your brain is cushioned by and floats around in this fluid, having low CSF causes a *massive* headache when sitting upright or standing. I've had frequent migraine headaches since I was a little kid, but that was no preparation for a CSF leak; I'd take a bad migraine over this "spinal headache" any day.

If I was lying completely flat, there was almost no pain at all. If I lay on pillows, which would raise my head a few inches off the bed, the pain began fading in slightly. When I sat all the way up, it felt like a million little knives were stabbing all over my head, and nausea quickly overcame my stomach. The longer I was upright, the bigger the pain and discomfort grew until I had to quickly lie back down again.

At first, they told me it'd only last a couple days and then would close up on its own. They gave me IV fluids right away, hoping that'd help, and then some Tylenol.

On the second day of this spinal headache, a physical therapist came in for the first time. I *was* in the hospital for my legs, after all.

First, the PT just instructed me to do various exercises in bed. I sat up slowly, bracing myself for the head pain to come back, then followed all of the

Jen

leg exercises she wanted me to do. Afterwards, I shifted over to sit at the edge of the bed as the PT wrapped an all-too-familiar gait belt around my waist. I sighed, remembering how I'd had to use a very similar ugly belt in the hospital three years prior, and I remembered how I'd quickly tried to get rid of it.

The PT put a plain, gray walker in front of me and instructed me to hold onto the handles to try to stand up. I did as told, and she helped both hold the walker in place and push me into a standing position. With the aid of the therapist and walker, I was able to stand for a bit and bear some weight on my legs, though they tired pretty quickly.

As the week went on, I continued to do physical and occupational therapy daily, going from standing to taking a few steps, and then slowly walking down the hallway with the assistance of the walker and the PT. Meanwhile, the OT assisted me with things like brushing my teeth while standing, which was a much harder feat than it sounds.

We noticed through my PT sessions that though I was beginning to be able to take fairly normal steps with my right leg (weak and slow, but close to normal stepping movement), my left leg dragged and I'd developed foot drop on that side. When taking steps with the walker, I had to put a lot of weight through my arms to lift my left leg at the hip and slide it forward.

Unfortunately, though, my spinal headache still wasn't getting any better. By the end of each PT session, not only were my legs—and arms, from having to actually put some weight through them—exhausted and achy, my head pounded. They gave me lots of fluids, Tylenol and Advil, and even caffeine pills to try to get rid of it, but none of that was very effective—the straight up caffeine was the most effective out of all of that, actually, but still, it only helped for about an hour.

They kept saying the next step for me was inpatient rehab at the Rehabilitation Institute of Chicago (RIC), but they wouldn't transfer me until the spinal headache was gone. As days passed, it became clear that it was taking forever to go away on its own.

It wasn't until a whole week after first arriving at this hospital that an anesthesiologist finally agreed to do a procedure called a blood patch to treat it.

I was wheeled down to a procedure room early in the morning of my last day in that hospital, where the anesthesiologist greeted me and re-explained the procedure, which he said should only take a few minutes. He first numbed my lower back with a local anesthetic, and a nurse drew some blood from my arm. Once my back was numbed, I braced myself for the needle poke in my back, where he was inserting my blood into the epidural space to "plug" the leak.

Surprisingly, it didn't hurt very much, which was a relief. This relief didn't last, though, as the room suddenly started spinning, and I grew increasingly nauseated and covered in cold sweat, which I guessed was just my body reacting to the sudden change in spinal fluid levels. I squeezed my eyes shut as the nurse slowly wheeled me to a recovery room, where she hooked my IV up to some Zofran for the nausea and then left me to rest for a bit.

Luckily, it wasn't long before I started feeling better… From both the blood patch *and* the spinal headache. The nurse brought me back up to my room, where my mom began to pack our things for my transfer to the Rehabilitation Institute of Chicago.

Up and Down

"Who'll get hurt, but who learns how to toughen up"

- *Waitress*, "She Used to Be Mine"

Sarah Todd

Eventually, I'd learned that it was impossible to have Transverse Myelitis and simply *have* it without any other ailments coming my way as a result. In the spring of 2015, I made the bold decision of auditioning for my school's musical. I hadn't performed in a proper show since I was a magic fairy in *Cinderella* less than a month before my life changed completely, and I knew things were going to be different. This wasn't a ballet, it was a musical, but they both carried similar challenges. There were numerous obstacles I had to take in account when I chose to participate; whereas a "normal" kid could simply audition, I could not. I had to consider how tired I might get during rehearsals and performances, how I was going to put on my costume and deal with quick-changes, how I was going to do my hair, and how I was going to do the choreography. It seemed dumb that I worried about the choreography, considering I'm a dancer, but I feared the audience members would assume I didn't know the correct choreography or that I was a bad dancer since I'd be adjusting the dances to fit my abilities. I loved standing out, but not when people didn't understand.

Up and Down

Once I'd auditioned and was assigned a part, rehearsals began. The schedule was rigorous, and I often didn't get home until eight o'clock in the evening. I was having a blast working on a piece of theatre; it felt satisfying to be working on a performance to share with an audience again. The choreography wasn't advanced by any means, and the director told me I could adjust it any way I needed to. Since choreography had become my thing, it was easy for me to manipulate the movements so they'd work for me, and I slowly forgot to care if people thought I wasn't doing the dance correctly. I knew I was, and that was all that mattered.

The rehearsals were stringent, and I was always pretty tired afterwards. It seemed like I was living at school; every morning, when I arrived on campus, I felt like I'd just left! I didn't mind the extra work, though—I'd had to do the same for ballet.

But things did get worrisome when my health started to deteriorate.

When I was walking upstairs to class one morning after rehearsals, my left leg wobbled, shaking slightly. With my right hand, I gripped the railing as tight as I could, scared I might fall. My breath was caught in my throat as I made my way up the remaining stairs, worried that something was seriously wrong. Whenever I have a health issue—even a minor one—I automatically assume it's something horrendous, like getting diagnosed with brain cancer when I have a headache, or even getting TM again despite the very slim chances of that happening. I always tried to tell myself these fears were irrational, but I couldn't get rid of them. After experiencing a life-altering disorder, it really didn't seem all that odd to me that I got paranoid about my health every once in awhile.

My leg felt normal for the rest of the day, save for when I went up or down stairs. Every time I did, the same unstable, wobbly feeling returned, making me anxious. I never put it past TM to bring on unusual symptoms, but I'd never experienced any quite like this. Numbness and tingling had become familiar to me, but not spontaneous weakness—especially in my legs. Even though I was worried, I told myself it would go away by tomorrow, just like the other weird symptoms TM generously gave me. Except it didn't, so I became even more worried the next day at school as I walked up the steps again. I reassured myself that this episode of weakness would go away soon, just like I'd done the day before, and made sure I was extra careful on the stairs.

At rehearsal that afternoon, we were working on our dances, and I struggled to keep up with the other cast members. My leg felt increasingly unstable as I participated in the choreography, and my body began to heat up with anxiety. I didn't want to sit out, because I wanted to keep up with everyone else and learn the choreography, but I'd started to struggle too much. Walking downstage towards the director, I paid close attention to my leg and moved slower than normal. The fear that I might fall still hadn't gone away, even throughout the whole day. I explained what was going on to the director, and he understood immediately, allowing me to sit and watch from the audience.

I'd always been accustomed to being *on* the stage, not off, so I felt out of place watching my friends dance on-stage. I knew I couldn't help that my leg wasn't working correctly, but the stubborn part of me was slightly angry with myself for giving up and sitting down. That wasn't like me. But I reminded myself that it was okay to stop, take a deep breath, and take a break every now and then, especially when my body was practically screaming at me to do just that.

The next day in drama class, we sat on the floor of the dance studio and watched videos for the entire class. I should've asked for a chair, but I didn't want to be a bother, so I sat on the floor with everyone else. It was easier to not have to ask for help—at least until I realized I really did need a chair. Without a chair, I ended up sitting so that my left leg was under my body since I was wearing a skirt. It wasn't the most comfortable position, but I felt that I could manage for the duration of the class. But when I stood up, my left leg nearly collapsed, reminding me of when I'd gotten out of the car at the urgent care center when I'd first gotten TM. Scared, I grabbed onto the ballet barre to steady myself, then told my friend what was happening.

"I don't think I can walk to the clinic," I told her, feeling the anxiety bubbling in my chest. The clinic was only right down the hall, but I didn't think I could even make it two steps. And that was just ridiculous. I was only thirteen years old, yet I wasn't confident that I could take two simple steps. "Can I hold onto your arm and have you walk with me there?" I asked her, hoping that would work. She, of course, agreed and helped me walk the short distance (that felt like a mile in my state) there. I knew the nurse at my school quite well, so she was very alarmed when I told her what was happening, but she couldn't figure out what was causing it. So I rested in the clinic for awhile until I needed to use the restroom, which I knew was going to be a challenge. How was I going to get there? It felt odd to have to worry about how I was going to get around, because mobility issues weren't usually an issue for me.

I told the nurse I needed to use the restroom, and when I stood up, my leg felt much better than before. It still didn't feel normal, but it didn't feel like a deadweight. The nurse helped me to the restroom by holding my arm, and I blushed as visitors in the front office stared at me and my wobbling leg. I did what I always do and smiled back at them, nearing the restroom slowly, happy when I made it there successfully. But I was still nervous, because although my leg seemed to be getting better, it still wasn't where it should be. The nurse had called my mom, who had my physical therapist, Michelle, come to my school to check on me and see what was going on. She moved my leg around and tested my muscle strength, and she said my muscle strength was the same, but my leg was definitely acting weaker than usual. I grew really alarmed at that, my mind of course drifting to the worst possible scenarios, but Michelle reassured me that I was most definitely not getting TM again. I knew that, of course, but the irrational thought always lingered. The cause of my weakness remained unknown, though, so by the end of the day, my parents decided to take me to the Emergency Room. It felt odd to get out of the car so slowly once we arrived at the ER because, well, we *were* at the Emergency Room. But this leg weakness wasn't an emergency compared to my past two experiences at the ER. At least, I didn't think it was. I hadn't been to the ER in five years (excluding the time I cracked open my chin), and it felt all too real. It wasn't enough that I'd gotten TM and was paralyzed—I also had to deal with frightening events like random, sudden weakness.

We didn't have to wait very long to be called back by a nurse, which was a surprise, and when we were, we simply explained the problem and listed off my medications. It was different actually being a part of talking to the nurses and doctors this time around; I was older, and so I was able to communicate more maturely. My communication skills really came in handy once I was given a room, because after waiting on a doctor, my nurse came in and asked me where I preferred having an IV. My true answer was nowhere, but I was confused as to why she was asking me this question in the first place.

"Why do I need an IV?" I asked her, my voice beginning to shake. I utterly despised IVs and blood draws. After having nurses try more than five times to get one IV in and having my blood spilled on me during a blood draw, these procedures had not left good tastes in my mouth.

"We're going to do an MRI," she explained, attempting to place a heat pack on my right arm, "to check on your leg."

Tears immediately gathered in my eyes. I knew I was thirteen and probably looked quite babyish, but IVs and MRIs did *not* sit well with me. "I'm not doing an MRI. I can't," I argued, looking to my parents for help. If I ever needed to have any major tests done, I always preferred knowing in advance so I could mentally prepare myself for what was to come. So having this sprung on me on the spur of the moment stressed me out. It sucked having to feel so afraid of tests and procedures that really shouldn't be big deals, but one bad experience has the power to override all the good ones.

Thankfully, the nurse sensed the tension in the room and left to retrieve one of the on-call neurologists, who came to assess my situation. She looked at both my legs and reiterated what Michelle had said: my muscle strength was the same, but my leg definitely was acting weaker. It was a relief to also have a doctor confirm that my muscle strength wasn't deteriorating, but that did make figuring out the cause of the weakness more difficult. The neuro, who we ended up liking very much, decided to try wrapping my left knee up with ace wrap so it couldn't collapse as easily. With the ace wrap on, I attempted to walk in the hospital hallway.

I'm basically learning how to walk yet again.

My knee still felt weak, but it didn't collapse as intensely or as often as it did earlier. My parents and neuro smiled as they watched me walk, clearly feeling a sense of relief even though the cause was still unknown. I, too, was relieved, but I wanted to know why my leg was acting up and how it could be fixed. I definitely didn't want to have to wear ace wrap around my knee forever, and I worried that I wouldn't be able to get back into the musical. I was already missing one rehearsal to go to the hospital, and I really didn't want to miss any more. I guessed this was my determination showing through yet again.

The neuro ended up releasing me from the ER shortly after I walked in the hallway. She said that my leg was most likely tired from working so hard on the musical and told me to just keep an eye on it. I trusted her and hoped she was right, because being able to dance and participate in the musical was extremely important to me. My health had gotten in the way of a lot of things, obviously, but I always managed to push through. And it was no different in this situation; I took things easy for awhile—walked slower around school, sat out during rehearsals if needed, danced with extra caution. It was weird to have to worry so much about my legs since all my attention was usually on my arms, but I was relieved to know that it most likely wasn't a big deal.

And it wasn't, really. Within a few more days, my leg was almost back to normal, save for a few slip ups when it wobbled slightly as I went up stairs or danced. Things like this had just become part of my life. Having Transverse Myelitis isn't *just* having Transverse Myelitis; there are too many other things that come along with it. But I just had to accept that I would have some hiccups every once in awhile and that not everything could always be perfect—especially when having a disability.

Up and Down

"Even the darkest night will end and the sun will rise"

- Les Miserables, "Finale"

Jen

Being at a rehab hospital is very different from being in a regular hospital. In some ways, the days are much busier because of all the therapy, but there are also a lot more freedoms.

As soon as I arrived at the Rehabilitation Institute of Chicago, I was brought up to a fairly large room on the 7th floor, which I learned contained the "Legs and Walking Lab." Though the building was relatively old (they were actually in the process of building a brand new building down the street to replace RIC), this floor had recently been renovated and was very new-looking, complete with a large gym with a ton of cool-looking therapy equipment. Supposedly, this floor was a glimpse of what the entire brand new rehab center would look like when it was completed, so I thought it was pretty cool that that's where I was living.

As soon as I got to my room, I noticed that there was a large window along the wall opposite the door, right beside my bed, which looked out on the city and Lake Michigan. It was a really nice day out, and from that height, there was a clear view of how the sun made the water sparkle. It really made me wish I could be outside.

The next thing I noticed was that I had a roommate. They hadn't had room for me on the pediatrics floor, but I was close enough to being an adult that it wasn't a big deal. Because of this, my roommate happened to be pretty far from my age—she was probably around her 50's—and she had recently had a brain tumor removed, so she had to relearn everything: speaking, walking, coordination, certain aspects of cognitive function. At first, I was annoyed that I had to have a roommate—especially since she had a habit of repeatedly clicking pens and her wheelchair seatbelt when bored—but she and her husband were very sweet, and I warmed up to her not too long after arriving.

As I settled in to my new room, a nurse came by with a schedule for the next day, which listed times for occupational therapy, physical therapy, and group PT/OT. She also brought me an actual wheelchair with a comfortable seat cushion and backrest for me to use while I was there in place of my flimsy transport chair. She then informed us that I could get a pass to leave for a couple hours each day if I wanted, which I was really happy about, knowing that some time away from the hospital would certainly make my time at RIC much easier. I was already very sick of staying inside a hospital all day, even after just a week.

••••

A lot of things happened during my first week at RIC. My first full day began bright and early as the occupational therapist came to assess me, followed by the physical therapist. At some point during those first few days, after they'd had a couple sessions to fully assess me and come up with a plan for my recovery process, we had a meeting with my main therapists, who wanted to keep me there for around three or four weeks. It was just an estimate, but I was a little annoyed, as I hadn't really expected to be there for more than a week.

I also had an EMG (electromyography) and nerve conduction test done during that first week. I'd heard about it a lot, both from other people with TM who'd had it done and from some of my own doctors over the years, so I knew what it was, but I'd never had it before now. I was told I would only need it done on my left leg, though, which I figured wouldn't be horrible.

When the doctor came in, I noticed that she was using a wheelchair, which I thought was cool to see. It's not like I ever doubted that someone with a disability could hold a job like a doctor—I knew it was possible, and happened—but there isn't much representation, and I'd never had a visibly disabled doctor, nurse, or therapist before. It was such a small thing, but still, it helped reinforce my desire to work in the medical field and made it even clearer that that would, in fact, be possible someday.

The EMG/nerve conduction test wasn't the worst thing I'd ever experienced, but it wasn't the most pleasant experience, either. They basically shocked my nerves and dug a needle into my muscles to see how well they functioned, which is really uncomfortable and pretty painful. After they were done doing it on my left leg, they decided to do it on my right one, as well, so they could compare them. They then wanted to do my arms, too, but at that point my legs were a bit sore, and I really wasn't in the mood for *all* of my limbs to be prodded, so they agreed to just leave it at that.

Meanwhile, my aunt made sure to visit me every day since she lived and worked much closer to RIC than we did. She tried to get me out of there for an outing pretty much every day either during a break in-between or after therapy sessions, and we frequently went places for dinner, Starbucks, or even shopped for a little bit at the Water Tower Place mall. Naturally, it was always the highlight of my days there.

• • • •

The gym where I did therapy on my floor had a crazy amount of equipment, including lots of machines whose functions were a complete mystery to me at first, but I eventually got to know and use many of them.

The machine that I probably used the most was a treadmill, which was basically a normal treadmill, except I was held up by a harness hanging from the ceiling. The harness kept me upright as the treadmill moved slowly, and my PT helped move my left leg to walk on it. To make this easier, they also gave me an AFO brace to wear in my shoe, which kept my ankle stabilized so my foot wouldn't drop and drag so much. This made it much easier to take steps.

Another machine I used a lot was a really cool anti-gravity treadmill called the AlterG. My PT helped me put these special shorts around my legs, which were made of a really tight, spandex-like material with a soft, plastic-y ring around the waist. I then had to stand in the middle of the treadmill, holding onto the bar in front of me for support, as the PT zipped the ring around my waist to the big plastic sheath surrounding the treadmill. After it was attached together by the zipper, the machine was turned on, inflating the plastic and entrapping my lower body in the tent. The air supported my legs and made them feel lighter, and the various settings on the treadmill could have allowed me to go anywhere from supporting 0% of my own weight to 100% of my own weight. It felt similar to walking underwater, like how the buoyancy of the water supports you, but without the weight of water slowing you down. I really loved that treadmill, because the weightlessness made walking so much easier—even though I was still pretty slow.

Therapy wasn't all about those machines, through. My main PT and OT also frequently tried to make therapy fun (or as fun as it could be) while I was there. Once, in PT, she had me play "basketball" with a giant orange yoga ball, in which she held onto me as I stood, then bounced the ball in front of me and had me try to dribble it while standing. I also played on the Wii during PT a couple times, where she'd have me stand with the walker in front of me and try to play Wii Sports games while standing. That was actually much more difficult than it sounds, and it got exhausting pretty quickly, but I had to admit, it was fun!

As for OT, one time we actually baked and decorated cookies together. There was a whole kitchen on another floor of the building where patients and therapists could bake or cook. I'd always loved baking and frequently did it at home, so I was excited to be able to bake in therapy. The "therapy" part of it was making me stand as much as I could while mixing ingredients and decorating the cookies, which, of course, was also exhausting and required sitting breaks, but it was fun. We also did arts and crafts in group OT sometimes, and once we spent the entire time drawing fall pictures. I drew a pretty, colorful leaf with oil pastels, which I gave to my roommate after that OT session ended. I definitely wasn't a great artist by any means, but I think she appreciated it, and I always liked making her smile.

• • • •

During that month of being in the hospital, I kept feeling like I was missing so much. When my friends came to visit, they filled me in on things happening at school, and it was crazy how much I was completely oblivious about due to not being at school. I also missed a bunch of cross country meets, of course, which I was always sad about; I missed my team so much. That year's Chicago Marathon occurred while I was staying at RIC and, knowing that a good portion of my cross country team was going to be there to volunteer, I begged my mom to bring me over to where they were stationed during my outing that day.

"Their stations are too far from us right now," my mom replied. "It's too cold to go over there. I'm sorry."

I was disappointed, but I knew it wouldn't be too long before I'd be out of here for good and could see them again at school. I hoped.

Another thing I was missing due to my hospital stay was that year's TM walk, which was a fun event every year for raising awareness for rare neuroimmunological disorders, and for raising money for the Transverse Myelitis Association.

I was really disappointed about missing that, as it had been awhile since I'd last seen a lot of those people, and I'd really enjoyed the walk the previous year. Most of my family still attended, though, and I saw pictures of them carrying signs with my name on them, which was slightly embarrassing, but also really sweet. I was glad they were still able to make it and had a good time!

I didn't have to feel left out for very long, though, because I got to have my own mini "TM Walk" in RIC, thanks to a certain visitor.

Trevor was someone who was a big part of the Transverse Myelitis community and had been a constant supporter of many people with TM over the years, including me. He was in the area for the TM walk and, knowing I was in the hospital, decided to come visit me afterwards. I was wearing my royal blue t-shirt from the previous year's TM walk, and Trevor arrived wearing not only a similar shirt from this year's walk, but also a giant blue tutu and tiara, which he'd apparently worn during the entire real walk.

After our "walk"—in which we just wheeled down the hall once or twice with the blue shirts—we talked for a little while until he had to leave. It was so nice to have the chance to meet such a great supporter in person, and it definitely helped me forget about being a little down about missing the walk.

Visitors were so great for that in general; it was always a breath of fresh air to see people other than the doctors, nurses, and therapists. It was also especially fun when my friends came to visit. A big group of them came once, and my outing that day consisted of them wheeling me through the streets of Chicago, stopping at Garrett's Popcorn and a cupcake shop for snacks and browsing through Eataly before returning to RIC. Another time, a different group of friends came and brought me to the mall, where we ate dinner and wandered through the shops a bit, then rushed back to the hospital as we realized we were cutting it very close to the "curfew" RIC had given me. My friends sprinted as they pushed me, and we could not stop laughing at the ridiculousness of the situation.

Every time, it was really sad to see them leave at the end of the day. I missed everyone terribly! But, luckily, the end of my time at inpatient rehab eventually came to a close. After about a month of living in hospitals, it was finally time to be discharged for good. I left with all of the sweet cards from my choir, cross country team, Best Buddies students, and various friends and family members (including a lot from my little siblings); the rest of my belongings; the rental wheelchair I was given to use before getting a custom one; and my very own brand-new, ugly silver walker, which allowed me to be able to walk short distances.

Jen

I was going to continue therapy for a couple more months through one of RIC's outpatient day rehab facilities, but at least I'd be home! By now, I could walk short distances with the walker and a couple steps without it, but I still needed the wheelchair a lot of the time. I hoped that would improve in outpatient therapy. I also hoped the new neurologist I was going to see in a couple weeks would be able to figure out why, exactly, my symptoms had worsened.

It had to be uphill from here.

Up and Down

Key Change

Up and Down

"I feel I've found myself, yeah, and I found my voice"

- *Pretty Woman: The Musical,* "I Can't Go Back"

Sarah Todd

When I was in kindergarten and first grade, I went to cheer camp over the summer and cheered for football in the fall. I absolutely adored cheering. I loved feeling pretty in my cheer uniform and doing cool tricks and jumps. It must've been the dancer in me. Since getting TM, I'd gotten back into dancing, of course, but I hadn't really considered getting back into cheerleading. But I worked for the school paper in seventh grade, and I interviewed the eighth grade cheerleaders for an article, which made me want to cheerlead again. I had to wait until eighth grade since seventh graders weren't allowed to cheer, but when try-outs were announced in May, I made sure to go.

Obviously my cheerleading abilities had changed since I last cheered, but I reasoned that if I could dance, I could cheer. Before tryouts, I met with one of the coaches and explained to her that I wouldn't be able to do certain things, like toe-touches and some of the arm motions. She told me that was perfectly okay. I was glad she was so accommodating so that I would be able to try out just like everyone else, but that didn't stop weird rumors from forming.

On the day of tryouts, I overheard one girl talking to a few other girls who were trying out.

"Sarah Todd has a guaranteed spot on the squad," she told them in a know-it-all tone. I felt myself go rigid. Obviously, that rumor wasn't true; I had to tryout just like everyone else besides the few exceptions I'd talked about with the coach. In the end, all of us who tried out made the squad (which wasn't unusual for eighth grade cheerleading), so the girl who started that rumor had no reason to worry about me making the squad in the first place. She had no reason to think I would automatically make the squad just because I had a disability. I actually felt like it was more difficult for me to make the squad, because I wasn't able to show the coaches my true potential since I couldn't do all the hand motions and jumps. But I tried to think of cheer how I do dance: my making up new, different arm motions for cheer was no different than my choreographing dances suitable for my body. Either way, I was just making the most of what I could do, which I'd gotten pretty good at since April 19, 2010.

And I really did end up incorporating my choreography skills in cheerleading. My coach met up with me that summer before the cheer season began and went over several cheers and motions with me. I watched her do the cheers first, then I did them myself with the adjusted arm motions I came up with. The process was very similar to adjusting the dances on my DVDs to suit my body, and my coach complimented my skill in coming up with easier motions.

"I'm a choreographer," I told her with a smile. "It's nothing new to me."

••••

On the same day as cheer tryouts, I also auditioned for my school's dance company. The tryouts and auditions coincided, so I auditioned after everyone else all by myself. Wearing my tights, leotard, and ballet slippers felt slightly foreign to me, because I hadn't dressed like a true ballerina since I performed "Adrift" the summer before, but it felt refreshing. It reminded me of attending auditions for shows when I was little, like *Swan Lake* and *Cinderella*, and how my stomach would swirl with excitement as I entered the studio, hoping I would get the part I wanted. My mom was a true "dance mom," as I remember she always stressed that I dance in the front row rather than in the back so I could be seen perfectly. I remember walking out of my *Swan Lake* audition when I was seven after dancing in the back row, and the first thing my mom said was, "You should've danced in the front so they could see you!" And this: I auditioned to be a gingerbread doll in *Babes in Toyland*, and I desperately wanted to be a gingerbread girl instead of a gingerbread boy. *Typical eight-year-old ballerina.* On the way to my audition, my mom coached me, "So how are you going to act if you're chosen to be a gingerbread boy and not a girl?" to which I replied, "Well, obviously I want to be a gingerbread *girl*, but if I'm a gingerbread boy, I'll still be happy." She just always wanted the best for me.

But during this audition, I didn't have to worry about standing in the very front row or whether or not I'd be cast in a male or female role. All I was focused on was earning myself a place in the company. I'd wanted to be a part of a dance company for as long as I could remember, and although this company wasn't with my old dance studio, it was still a dance company I could be a part of.

Dancing on an actual, real stage made me feel giddy inside, because I hadn't danced on one since I performed "Adrift" at camp the year before. I followed all of the dance instructor's directions throughout the audition, performing all the correct moves she asked of me to the best of my ability. And while I was dancing, I realized I wasn't even worried about how my arms looked; I performed the motions just as I did when choreographing my own dances, feeling confident. And I carried that confidence with me until the very end of my audition when I spoke with another one of the dance instructors. She had taught me ballet at my old dance studio, but I hadn't danced with her since I got TM, so she asked me some questions about my abilities and movement. I didn't have any qualms with that until she made one comment that made me furious.

"We'll probably have to put you in the back if you dance with us," she said so casually, like she hadn't just blatantly insulted me or my dance ability. I just nodded along, but on the inside, I was trembling with anger. I'd been dancing since I was three years old, and my having a spinal cord injury did not make me any less of a dancer. Her wanting to put me in the back like she would be embarrassed to have me dance as a part of the company infuriated me. I knew that I was just as good of a dancer as the other girls. My unique dance style I discovered because of my disability helped me express myself even better as a dancer—something that the other girls didn't have.

Since I became a dancer with a disability, I learned that part of what makes dance so beautiful is that there are no rules. Sure, there's first position, second position, third position, etc., turn out, pointed feet… but dance truly can be whatever a dancer desires for it to be. My arms weren't able to conform to the typical moves and positions of dance, but I was still a dancer. It saddened me that even a ballet instructor could not distinguish the true beauty in that.

And a week later when I received an email explaining that, because I was also participating in cheerleading, the dance company would not be able to offer me a spot, I knew I'd wasted my time. They shouldn't have had me audition anyway.

Up and Down

"Even if the time gets tough and the road is long, you don't have to be lonely"

- Mandy Gonzalez, "Smile"

Jen

"Hey, Angela and I are going to get coffee after school tomorrow! Do you want to come?" my friend, Jaime, asked me just a couple days after I'd been discharged. I smiled and agreed, happy about the chance to spend some time with a couple of my closest friends after not seeing them for so long.

Since the plan was that we'd meet at Jaime's house before heading over to the small coffee shop downtown, my mom drove me over there the next day. It was only late afternoon, but since it was nearing the end of October, it was already getting dark.

As soon as we arrived, Jaime and her dad met us outside.

"We're going to hang out at my house for a little bit before going!" she told me. "My dad will help get you in the house through the back."

I was a little confused as to why we were going through her back door, or why we weren't just going straight to the coffee shop, but I didn't think too much of it. Her dad lifted me in my chair to get me over the few steps to the porch leading to the back door.

"SURPRISE!"

As soon as we got into the house, a huge group of of my friends jumped out and flipped the lights on, all of them beaming. I now noticed that the kitchen was decorated with a huge, handwritten sign that said: "WELCOME HOME, JEN!" The kitchen table was covered with a colorful tablecloth and full of snacks. We weren't going to get coffee, after all; instead, they had set up a welcome home surprise party for me! I was so grateful to have such supportive friends.

That party ended up being amazing. We talked a ton and I got caught up on everything that had been going on in their lives the past month. We also took a lot of cute and silly pictures, sang songs while a couple of them played their guitars, and then played games for hours, having a generally amazing time talking, laughing, and enjoying each other's company. It was so nice to see all of my friends together again, and I couldn't thank them more for such a sweet, unforgettable welcome back to life at home.

• • • •

Diving back into my junior year of high school was a little bit of an adjustment, but for the most part, it just made life feel normal again. Since I couldn't wheel this wheelchair very far by myself, though, and certainly couldn't walk far with my walker, either, I had to work it out with my friends to push me around to all of my classes. They'd always been helpful in general, but they'd never had to help me *this* much in the past. I tried to keep it as light as possible for them by alternating friends each class period, but still, I hated having to rely on people for something as simple as moving around. It quickly grew frustrating to have to ask whoever was pushing me to change direction if needed.

Luckily, this eventually changed when I got my own custom chair. The process took a little while, which was a bit annoying, but it was worth it.

I first had to have a seating clinic appointment at RIC, where they took measurements and assessed me to determine what exactly I needed for my chair. Because my arms weren't strong enough (and the grip on my right hand not quite good enough) to use a fully manual wheelchair all the time, we had to explore our other options.

Originally, what I really wanted was a manual chair with power assist wheels. Basically, it's a regular, lightweight manual chair with special electronic wheels that amplify each "push" movement, so not as much strength is needed to operate them. A tiny push on those wheels can act as a normal-sized push, and there are a couple different settings for the wheels depending on how much amplification you need, and you can have a different setting on each side if needed.

While we talked about options, they thought that could potentially be a good fit for me. They had various types of wheelchairs there at the facility for people to test out, so they found one with the power assist wheels for me and adjusted the wheels so that the right side had more amplification than the left. I then went out into the hall to try it out.

The hallway on that floor just formed a big circle, so they encouraged me to try a whole lap. I gave the wheels a light "push," which sharply threw me forward and to the right. They took some getting used to, clearly, but I was determined to get the hang of them.

But, though I was sort of getting the hang of it, it quickly became clear that they weren't going to be the right fit for me. By the time the one lap was over, my arms had become too fatigued and achy from that constant, repetitive movement to push for much longer, which wouldn't work because I, of course, wanted to be able to keep up with my friends for any distance! Also, even though the settings for each wheel were different, I was having a hard time not veering towards the right side due to my left arm being so much stronger than the other.

Next, they had me test out a fully motorized wheelchair, which was nice because I could go really fast and move for as long and as far as I wanted since the only work I was doing was moving my left hand to push a joystick around. I was still disappointed, though, since I was kind of afraid of the bulkiness and weight of the fully motorized wheelchair; I wanted to keep up with my friends, but I also wanted it to be able to fit in their cars (or at least some of their cars). But then the people at the seating clinic had an idea that'd be almost like a compromise.

They told me that another option they had was a joystick attachment for a manual chair. It was similar to the power assist wheels in that they'd fit me for a regular manual wheelchair of some sort, and then add special wheels that connected to a joystick, which would attach to the left armrest, and a battery underneath, which would power everything. They brought the model out for me to see, and I wasn't able to test theirs out because it wasn't charged, but it looked like a good fit for what I needed, so I ultimately agreed to that one.

It was a few months before I was able to bring my custom chair home, but finally, that spring of my junior year, it was ready! It was nice to be able to ditch the pillow behind my back for the customized backrest that had good lumbar support (because otherwise, my back hurt really quickly), and the seat cushion was way more comfortable than what I'd been using temporarily. I zoomed around the floor of the seating clinic at RIC, getting used to the feel of it and savoring my newfound freedom.

Up and Down

"And pain gets hard, but now you're here, and I don't feel a thing"

- One Direction, "If I Could Fly"

Sarah Todd

Not many people can relate to living life with only one hand. There are so many things we don't even think about that require the use of two hands. My grandma always tells me that whenever she does something that requires both of her hands, she can't help but think of me. But I feel like most people don't truly think of me as someone who can only use one hand because I have two hands. I'm not an amputee, so the fact that I live life every day with only one hand never crosses anyone's mind because it's not noticeable. My one-handedness is very similar to that of an amputee's, though, even though there are several things that are easier for me to do since my left hand is still a part of my body, like holding a piece of paper down while I write. Even though not many people could relate to living life with only one hand, *Soul Surfer* Bethany Hamilton could.

I'd always identified with Bethany Hamilton after watching her movie because I realized just how similar we are to each other. We're both one handed, but in different ways. Bethany does have the advantage of her right arm functioning normally, while I have the advantage of having my left hand as a part of my body still, but that didn't take away from our ability to bond.

Bethany was someone I'd always wanted to meet, because she showed me that I would be able to do anything I aspired to do, and our similarities helped me feel like she understood me. And in October 2015, I had the opportunity to meet her, spend the day with her at the beach in San Clemente, and have lunch together! When she first walked onto the beach to meet me, she sent me the biggest smile. I couldn't wait to get to know her and learn some of her one-handed tips and tricks. It crossed my mind that she'd driven herself to the beach, and with only one hand. I wondered if that would be me someday: driving to meet up with friends or family with only one hand. That thought made me jittery.

We hung out and chatted for a while, taking pictures and having fun. I asked her how she does her hair with one hand, and she showed me how she wrapped it around her wrist and threw it up into a messy, but pretty, bun. I knew I couldn't reach my head like she could, but watching her do her own hair encouraged me to try it sometime.

"Adam, my husband, can also braid my hair," she told me proudly. "So that helps, too." My dad and brothers could *never* braid hair. There was just something about males and doing hair that didn't mix. My mom tried to teach my dad how to braid my hair once, and he did a pretty decent job, but it was kind of messy. Bethany was very lucky to have a hair-braiding husband like Adam! I'll most likely have to find one of those someday, too!

I got to watch Bethany surf the waves of Moonlight Beach after we chatted, and she made it look so easy. She turned super fast, and she caught a ton of waves. It felt so surreal to actually watch her surf in person. I'd only ever seen her surf through a screen, and seeing her surf in person was even more incredible. We lounged on the beach for awhile after she took on the waves and talked about her little baby son. I got to meet him at lunch after we hung-out on the beach, and he was the cutest thing. It was sweet to watch Bethany be a mom and hold her baby, and it made me wonder if I'd ever be able to hold my baby if I have one someday. I wondered what it would be like to be a mom with the way my body was. Being a mom with only one hand sounded difficult, but Bethany proved it was possible. She told me she could even change diapers with one hand!

Bethany had heard about my book, *5k, Ballet, and a Spinal Cord Injury*, so she was also super excited when I gave her a signed copy at lunch. We took a picture together with her holding up my book, and I smiled so widely. I couldn't believe it! Bethany Hamilton, who was defying the odds and living her life with one hand—just like me—had my book! It was an unforgettable day.

• • • •

It was Make-A-Wish Georgia's twentieth anniversary in 2015, so for their annual Wish Ball, they invited twenty of their most impactful Wishes to attend. And I was one of them! I got to wear a beautiful, ivory colored dress I picked out and parade with a sign that said my Wish was to meet One Direction. I'd never attended a cocktail party before, being only fourteen, so it was quite special getting to attend such a cool event.

Even a year later, I still thought about my Wish every day and constantly talked about it any chance I could get. Not only did I still think about my Wish, I knew Harry was still thinking about it, too. Two months earlier, when I was in Baltimore for my medical appointments, I went to the One Direction concert at the stadium there. My mom was able to get us seats right next to the catwalk that connected the main stage and the mini stage, so I essentially had a front row view! It was August 8, 2015, just nine days shy of my one-year Wish anniversary. And Harry Styles *still* spotted me in the crowd. He constantly waved at me, gave me peace signs and thumbs up, and smiled throughout the entire concert. I was *so* happy. He'd met so many other people and done so much since I'd met him, yet I'd made a big enough impact on him that he remembered me. I truly believed he had read my book and my letter, and the thought made me teary. There was no way he would've been able to remember me if he hadn't.

As if the constant attention from Harry wasn't enough, during "Story of My Life," he walked all the way back to the main stage and grabbed a towel. He walked back to the catwalk with it, then put it in his back pocket when it was his turn to sing. After his part was over, he turned around and came back to my side of the catwalk, kissed the towel, and then bent down right in front of me.

He pointed at me with the towel and mouthed "for you," making my heart stop. My mom pointed to me and checked, "her?" to which he nodded and pointed at me again. He lightly tossed the towel towards me, my mom catching it. Of course, I immediately burst into tears and gave my mom a hug. Harry had to go back to singing, but when he was done, I yelled "thank you!" at him, and he smiled, nodded, and gave me a big thumbs up.

I knew it was just a towel. But the point is: Harry remembered me and wanted to let me know it by doing something kind for me. He had no prior knowledge that I was going to be at that concert, and he knows I live in Atlanta, not Baltimore, so how he picked me out in a crowd of 80,000 fans is beyond me.

But it is an incredible story to tell.

Harry is a person who truly cares about people, and I know I'm one of those people. My Wish was to meet him and the rest of the band, but he has turned that one Wish into so much more. And I want people to know that. Harry Styles and I have the most special relationship he doesn't have with any other fan; he enjoyed meeting me as much as I enjoyed meeting him. And that's the power of a Wish.

Up and Down

"I'm through accepting limits 'cause someone says they're so"

- *Wicked*, "Defying Gravity"

Jen

My mom was the one who introduced me to the Great Lakes Adaptive Sports Association, which was a local organization that offered a bunch of different adaptive sports for disabled people. I had really been missing running and just generally being a part of a sport, so she had the idea to introduce me to adaptive sports since she'd heard about the organization and that it was really good.

My parents brought me to a building with a large gym, where I met a lady named Cindy, the head coach of GLASA. She discussed sports with me and, knowing that I was a runner, she wanted me to try out wheelchair track.

We entered the gym, and some other people from GLASA brought out a bunch of racing chairs and had me try one out. I got out of my own wheelchair and they helped me sit in the track chair's little black seat. The metal sides hugged my hips snugly, and my legs rested on a small foot plate below. When I was upright, I was simply in a normal sitting position, but I quickly found that I couldn't sit upright for very long before the lightweight chair started tipping backwards.

They then removed a pair of thick, black glove-like things out of one of the cardboard boxes sitting by the line of different colored track chairs by the back wall. The gloves loosely resembled a pair of small boxing gloves, and they slid them on my hands, then pulled on the Velcro near my wrists to tighten them. I was instructed to lean forward, and they showed me how to push the chair.

The gloves were made of a tough material, and basically, you have to "hit" the rims of the wheels to push them; the nice thing was, this didn't require any sort of grip. The wheels' rims were thin and small, the wheels thin, and the chair itself very light. When you're at that bent-over angle, it's actually surprisingly easy to make the chair move forward—especially on the smooth linoleum of the gym. It was far easier than pushing a regular manual wheelchair, that was for sure.

I slowly made my way to the other side of the gym, one of the GLASA coaches holding onto the back of the track chair the whole time—both to ensure that I didn't tip over and to help keep my momentum going—as I figured out how to push the wheels with uneven arm function.

But, I found this first chair incredibly uncomfortable and awkward; it was difficult to lean forwards and push when I was in that seated position, and the pain in my legs and back immediately increased. By the time I got back to the first side of the gym, my thighs and back were aching.

So, they helped me switch to a different type of racing chair. This one was red and yellow in color, and it was designed so that my legs were folded underneath me instead of being in front of me. Immediately, I found that I preferred this design, and I had a great time flying down the smooth hallway with it.

They let me take that chair home, and I was more than ready to try "running" track again.

• • • •

Doing track with GLASA was cool, but I also really wanted to compete on my school's track team with my friends and old coaches again. Luckily, GLASA knew how to make that happen. They came over to my high school one day to meet with the head coach of our track team, and they spent a lot of time educating him on wheelchair track and teaching him the logistics of the chair. My coach was more than receptive; he was *very* enthusiastic about everything.

I started track that spring, the spring of my junior year. Unlike most of my teammates, I didn't practice every single day because it was too exhausting for me. Instead, I usually practiced with my high school team a couple days a week, only competing with them during home meets, and I practiced with GLASA around once a week during the weekend.

At the high school meets, there was usually only one other person using a track chair, and she wasn't even there every single time, so I was always either racing against myself, or just one other girl (who was way faster than me!). This felt a little embarrassing, and I didn't really like when they gave me "first" or "second" place medals in these instances because it almost felt like a joke—of course you'll always get first place when you're the only one in the race!

Still, it was really, really fun to spend time with my friends and coaches, and I always enjoyed feeling like an athlete. I ended up making it to the State track meet because the first two runners of each race qualify (and, after all, there were only two of us), successfully fulfilling my high school goal of going to State at least once. Besides the three others on the team who qualified, Jaime also accompanied us down to the State meet, because she'd been the biggest help to me during that entire season of track! She was always the one helping me get into the track chair—which was near-impossible to do alone, at least for me—and helping me get my glove-things on. She always assisted me in my warm-ups and was one of my biggest sources of encouragement. I both wanted and needed her to be there with me, and I was so excited that she was able to come!

Though I didn't do great in the actual races themselves, State was still an amazing time. I loved getting to watch my friends from my team compete in their own races and do so well; it was cool to have the chance to cheer them on. We also had a ton of fun outside of the meet, like playing crazy games of "Heads Up" outside our hotel and braiding our coach's hair. We had a lot of laughs and memories that I don't think any of us will ever forget. That kind of camaraderie was always the best when being a part of a team.

A few weeks after the State meet came the GLASA Regionals Games. At GLASA meets, everyone was disabled in some way, which made me feel a lot less like an outcast on the track. Some were ambulatory runners, but many others were wheelchair runners as well. I still often trailed behind most people because it seemed like the majority of the other wheelchair runners had really strong arms (or at least averagely strong arms), which gave them a bit of an edge over me, but that is exactly why classifications exist in disabled sports.

Adaptive sports classifications are different for each sport, but overall, they're just a way of grouping disabled athletes based on their level of function. I had to be classified before competing in Regionals, and to do so, a lady thoroughly evaluated the function of my arms and core (and legs a little bit, but they weren't as relevant to this specific sport since I was using a track chair), and then watched me actually push and turn the chair before assigning me to a class.

At Regionals, you can qualify for something called the National Junior Disability Championships, a national event with a lot of different disabled sports in which those ages 22 and under who qualify within their sport and classification can compete. I ended up qualifying, and even though I didn't end up having the chance to go that year, it still felt like a big accomplishment.

Up and Down

"Give me therapy, I'm a walking travesty, but I'm smiling at everything"

- All Time Low, "Therapy"

Sarah Todd

I'd never danced in my front yard in over ninety-degree heat before, and I'd *also* never worried about tripping on rocks or sticks or stepping in a hole while dancing. As I did a jump, I forgot to pay attention to where I was landing, and I stumbled slightly when my feet touched the ground. But I kept dancing, knowing we could just cut that part out since we were filming three different times from three different angles. Every time I looked at my feet, I inwardly fretted about wearing my ballet slippers outside, but I knew the sacrifice was worth it for creating a meaningful dance. Sweating was a normal part of dancing, too, but not quite this much. I hadn't ever been so overheated while dancing before, but my front yard was the perfect location for my new self-choreographed dance.

I wanted it to be creative. Mental health awareness was incredibly important to me, and that's what the premise of my dance was. I wanted people to watch my dance and step away and think about how they could help those with mental illnesses. And in order for people to truly be impacted by it, it needed to be creative.

Throughout my dance entitled "Therapy," I hold up signs, each with different words: I'm, Sad, Alone, Angry, Fine. I start by sitting on the ground with a notebook in my lap, and I look at it in disgust before throwing it to the side, symbolizing my frustration with being unable to write out my feelings. A minute later, though, I pick the notebook back up again and flip through the pages, scrambling to find a blank one. Once I do, I begin to write, starting with "I'm." Then I dance with the sign with the word I wrote on it before I throw it to the ground and write another word on a different blank piece. "Sad," "Angry," and "Alone" were all the true emotions I and many others with mental illness had most likely felt—the very same ones I was too scared to share with anyone else. "Fine" was the most powerful word on a sign in "Therapy," which is why I purposely stared at the camera for a few seconds while holding up the word. I wanted people to look into my eyes while I held up the word "Fine" and see that I, in the dance, truly was not fine. At the very end of the dance, I throw the last sign on the ground, and it lands with all the others, symbolizing the terrible truth that not many people with mental illness speak out. In "Therapy," I'd felt sad, alone, and angry, but "fine" was the only word anyone heard or focused on.

    I've always been a deep thinker, and I love learning new things and sharing my thoughts with others. I suppose my interest in writing combined with a strong desire to speak out culminated in creating what became "Therapy." All Time Low sings the original song, but I performed to the instrumental in order to bring more attention to the dance and its message. When awareness can be brought to an important subject through enthralling art forms, people are much more likely to watch, listen, and just take everything in.

I was exhausted after performing the dance three times in the sweltering heat, so it felt relieving to sit and relax in a comfy chair when we were done filming while Jen and I edited the dance. My left arm felt extremely weak, but I *had* practiced "Therapy" a few times inside before performing it three times in extreme heat, so I wasn't too worried about it—it was probably just tired. Jen had filmed me performing "Therapy" all three times at a different angle each time, so it took some doing to figure out which angles were the best for each move I made in the dance. But once we decided which ones we liked, it wasn't too terribly difficult to put all the clips together. I was in awe when we watched the complete video for the first time. I knew this was my greatest self-choreographed dance yet. Every move I made flowed so well, my steps fluid and strong. My technique had definitely improved, alongside my choreography skills.

I was anxious to share "Therapy" with my mom for the first time. We'd discussed my past mental health issues briefly, but I hadn't ever felt comfortable being so open about it until I choreographed this dance. I didn't want her to think anything was wrong or cause her to worry, because I'd been so much happier ever since I met 1D. While "Therapy" was, indeed, a very personal dance, it was also a very informational one that needed to be shared, so

I of course shared it with her. She was amazed with my creativity and choreography as always, and I expected nothing less!

• • • •

When I woke up the next morning, my left arm felt like deadweight. It usually feels a little heavier than my right arm since my left doesn't move from my forearm down, but this feeling was not normal—even for me. I'd thought that it was just tired from all the dancing I did the day before, but I wasn't too sure about that theory now. If it were just overworked, I didn't think it'd *still* feel weak the next day—and not just weak, *weaker*. I got out of bed and tried lifting it up, and it felt like my arm was made of steel; I could still lift it, but it was incredibly difficult. My whole body grew hot, anxiety bubbling up in my chest, but I patiently tried again. This time, I couldn't lift my arm as high as I normally could, and it felt even heavier.

This was not good.

I immediately woke Jen up and told her what was going on.

"Are you sure it's not just tired?" she asked hopefully, though I could tell she wasn't very confident that was the case.

"I don't know," I told her, my voice shaky in panic. "I don't think it would be *this* hard to move if it was just tired." For emphasis, I attempted to lift my arm again, and it only proved to be even more difficult. Every time I tried to use it, my muscles tired out, making my arm feel increasingly heavy and more like a deadweight.

About three months earlier, in the beginning of March, I'd noticed that I was having trouble turning my left wrist over. My left wrist didn't have any movement, but I was always able to use some accessory muscles to flip it over, which helped me wash myself in the shower, carry heavy plates, carry my phone on my palm, and so much more (kind of like a tray). My left thumb also tingled when my arm was dangling at my side for more than a minute, and beginning that past September, my legs started growing tired quickly when I stood. I'd even started requiring a chair at my chorus concerts at school even though I'd been able to stand during them the year before. There was no explanation for that tingling and weakness, either, but it hadn't taken any of my independence away—it just felt a tiny bit weaker. Now, though, I was beginning to think this arm weakness was somehow connected to my faux wrist weakness, and I *was* losing independence.

My doctors and mom had talked about correcting my scoliosis through a spinal fusion surgery since August 2015 since the curve in my neck had gone haywire. I'd even visited a doctor at Johns Hopkins then to discuss surgery, but I wasn't interested at all. But around February 2016, the pain in my neck was becoming unbearable. It was a constant pain—nothing made it feel better. I never took Tylenol or used a heat pad, because truly, *nothing* made it feel better. It began to come clear to me that the only thing that could *potentially* cure my neck pain was a spinal fusion surgery, and there was no guarantee that I'd come out of surgery with a completely straight neck and back and never have neck pain ever again. Despite the possibility of the spinal fusion not curing my neck pain, I became very interested in pursuing the surgery simply because there was a chance it would help. Knowing my neck and back would look much straighter for sure was comforting, even if the surgeon wasn't able to make them completely straight. At least then, the surgery wouldn't be done for nothing.

I was beginning to wonder if my left wrist and arm weakness and reduced leg strength was from my scoliosis. "Mom, can you call Dr. B and ask him what he thinks?" I asked my mom, feeling the anxiety creeping into my chest. I *hated* when I didn't know what was going on. I always thought of the worst.

"He says your symptoms are not 'typical of scoliosis,'" she ended up telling me after she hung up the phone. We were both frustrated. It was obvious that these weren't typical symptoms, but my scoliosis wasn't typical, either. I had cervical scoliosis; most people have thoracic.

I hated not having answers. Everything about my TM compared to most cases was already so complicated, and it seemed like everything else that came along with it was unheard of and complex, too. Nothing about me or my disability was ever simple; no one ever had the answers we needed or knew just how to help right away. It was incredibly frustrating—infuriating, even.

Since my local neurosurgeon had no answers, I went through the rest of the days Jen was staying at my house losing my independence. I couldn't hold a bar of soap in my left palm and rub it against my right to get my hands soapy in the shower. I couldn't carry the big, glass plates we use in our kitchen with my left hand under the plate and my right hand on top like I had learned to do. Even while we were doing something as simple as taking pictures, I couldn't put my left hand on my hip or put my left arm around Jen's back.

Living with a disability was one thing, but losing independence I'd already lost and regained because of that disability was another.

• • • •

Once I succumbed to the fact that I really did need to have a spinal fusion, I was on a mission to discover the best surgeon to perform my surgery. Previously, I started in Atlanta, where I saw an orthopedic surgeon and a neurosurgeon. Then, shortly after Jen left my house to go back to Chicago and my left arm began losing function, my mom and I embarked on a week-long medical trip to visit other potential surgeons in the Northeast. We flew in to Philly and then drove a rental car to Wilmington, Delaware, where I saw an orthopedic surgeon, Dr. Shah, who had operated on the son of my mom's best friend several times. He wouldn't guarantee that surgery would cure my neck pain (and neither would the other doctors I saw, as my mom and I would soon learn), but he reasoned that it would most likely help—if not completely, then at least a little bit.

At one point, he asked me how I would feel if I had the operation and it didn't help my pain. "That would suck," I told him honestly, then blushed as everyone in the room laughed.

"The honest words of a fourteen-year-old," my mom said, shaking her head and laughing.

After we saw Dr. Shah, we drove to Baltimore so I could have an MRI to send to all the surgeons and see Dr. Sponseller, who I'd seen the previous August. Like everyone knows, I *despise* MRIs, so I, of course, was not looking forward to having one. IVs are also something I despise (mostly because of my horrifying experience with my MRI in 2012), so I chose to be sedated through a mask instead. I'd usually done much better with the mask, but for some reason, I had a lot of trouble relaxing and taking in the medicine this time. For about one minute, I felt like I was paralyzed from the neck-down again, and I tried calling out for help, but no one heard me. Afterwards, I asked my mom about it, and she said that she and the doctors had no idea I was trying to ask for help. I decided I was never going to be sedated through the mask again after that.

After Baltimore, we drove back to Philly, where we saw another orthopedic surgeon at Philly Shriner's. At each visit, my mom took notes, and we both asked several questions to help us choose the best surgeon. At home, I put all our notes into a spreadsheet, which helped me compare each of the surgeon's ideas. It was crazy to think that once I'd chosen a surgeon, I would be putting all my confidence and trust in him to repair my spine. I hoped it would work out.

"Turn up the music so loud that it swallows us whole"

- *Bring it On: The Musical*, "One Perfect Moment"

Jen

Every fall, Tri-M (music honors society) put on an event called Cabaret Night, which was basically a small, music-related talent show hosted in our choir room. Most people sang something, whether that be in a group or a solo, while some others played instruments. The event was always a hit, which was good, because its purpose was to raise money through ticket sales for a cause in the community. In Tri-M, we chose a different cause each year and, when we ended up splitting it into two nights instead of just one due to the number of people wanting to perform and watch, we had two different causes for each night. I loved how we were able to give back and make a difference through music.

I had always gone to Cabaret Night to watch and support my friends and classmates, who were always *incredible*; the amount of musical talent in my high school really showed through this event. I'd never performed at it before, though, because even though I'd always enjoyed music and singing, and my love for it was just continuing to grow bigger and bigger over time, I lacked a bit of confidence; it's hard to get up in front of people! But, this changed senior year, when four friends and I came up with a plan to do something as a group for Cabaret Night.

Jaime had come up with the idea initially and ended up inviting the rest of us into it. Her idea was to do a mashup of two songs, "I Was Made for Loving You" and "Please Don't Say You Love Me." We divided up parts in the song so each of us had a mini solo and, when we were all singing together, three of us made up a little harmony while the other two sang the melody. We also had Jaime tapping the beat on a box drum while one of the other girls played the guitar as an accompaniment (while the remaining three of us "just" sang while sitting there, which was honestly enough multi-tasking for me!).

We practiced it for weeks, and finally, it was time for the low-key auditions for Cabaret Night. It was just in front of our choir teacher in a practice room, but I was still a little nervous. But—as expected, considering we were some of her "favorites"—she *loved* it, so much that she wanted us to perform both of the nights.

"Okay, it's getting really close to when we need to go back in there! One more time?" Jaime said, the five of us sprawled out on the linoleum in the hallway outside the choir room, trying to get a little extra, last-minute practice in.

The rest of us agreed, and we practiced one final time before we had to do it for real. It was absolutely perfect! One of the others even accidentally added a high harmony at the end, which sounded really good, so we told her to keep doing that.

When it came time for the actual performance, though, I was *incredibly* nervous. I knew my tiny, ten-second "solo" in the middle of our song wasn't a big deal, but still, it was my first time singing any sort of solo—even a ten-second one—in front of people. The other four girls in my group there were way more musically experienced.

But it ended up going really, really well on both nights that we performed. After it was over, a lot of people from the audience complimented us, and I couldn't be prouder of our little group.

It marked so much: my confidence, my love for music. I began to realize just how much music and singing meant to me, and I knew that I'd be okay without running. There was actually a huge variety of things that made me happy, I was beginning to realize, and I couldn't wait for the chance to sing or enjoy amazing musical performances again.

• • • •

Not long after Cabaret Night, I decided to get back into adaptive sports again, because although I was enjoying throwing myself into music through three different choirs through my school that year (treble choir, plus treble jazz and mixed jazz choirs), I still wanted to do some sort of sport occasionally. Even if it was just once a week.

I didn't really want to do wheelchair track again, though. It had been pretty exhausting, and though I'd been excited about qualifying for the National Junior Disability Championships, I found that I didn't really love the sport in a chair even close to the way I'd loved running with legs. I had kind of been trying to "replace" running, in a way, which obviously didn't work. It was going to be different, and I knew that instead of trying to replace it, I had to accept that I could still hold a love for real running while making room for other things I could love, as well.

I noticed that one of the other sports that GLASA offered was adaptive swimming, which immediately appealed to me. From the time I was a little kid, I'd always liked to swim, and though I'd never been on a swim team or anything before, I remembered how I'd always kind of wanted to try that out! That was a long time ago, and until then, I'd completely forgotten about that childhood desire, but though I was now 18 years old, I knew it wasn't too late to fulfill it.

The next season of GLASA swim began that February, so that's when I started. Immediately, they started teaching me the different swim strokes, which included helping me figure out a way to do each stroke that worked with my disability. There was pretty much no way I'd be able to do Butterfly, because it required a lot of shoulder mobility and strength; I attempted it once, but it was clear it wouldn't work. I was fine with that, though, because I was still able to do all of the others, and Fly seemed to be most people's least favorite, anyway.

I picked up on everything pretty quickly, and it became clear almost immediately that I would really enjoy it—never as much as running, but closer than I ever would have expected. It was so much easier to move around in the water than on land, and swimming was so much easier on me than any other type of physical activity.

Though I never ended up competing in swim that year since I didn't feel quite ready, I knew it was something I would stick with, and I hoped I'd find a way to continue it in college.

Up and Down

"Must this hurt you just before you go?"

- Harry Styles, "Ever Since New York"

Sarah Todd

Ever since my mom took me to New York for spring break in 2015, the vibrant city had become my favorite place to visit. We'd planned a trip for July 2016, and every day we were there was packed with tours, restaurant reservations, and Broadway shows. My favorite tour we did was the *Gossip Girl* tour, where a tour guide took us on a bus to all the sites where episodes of the TV show were filmed. We even stayed at the Palace Hotel, where the characters go often to hang-out in the courtyard! I was *that* teenage girl: the one who wanted to stay in a specific hotel just because one of her favorite TV shows was filmed there. That tour was easy for me to keep up with since we were mostly on the bus, but my seemingly deteriorating body didn't want to cooperate with me during other activities. We had to skip our tour of the MET because I could hardly walk. My legs hurt after walking for only a couple minutes, and my left arm dangled like a deadweight, and my left thumb went numb and tingled.

"I could get a wheelchair there for you," Mom offered, but I refused. I couldn't believe that I'd been walking with no trouble for the past six years, yet we were back to a point where we considered getting me a wheelchair. Why was my body betraying me?

We ended up having to cancel our Greenwich Village Pizza Tour, too, and we didn't go to the 5 Seconds of Summer concert at Madison Square Garden either. Every night when we were walking to a show, my left thumb tingled, my arm dangled heavily by my side, and my legs ached, feeling like I'd run a marathon. I didn't understand. Just a little over a year before, I'd walked all over New York City without getting tired at all, and now I could barely walk for ten minutes to get to the theatres. This trip was turning out to not be as fun as fun as our previous one all because my body was failing me. I kept feeling like I'd ruined our trip because we'd cancelled so many fun things, but my mom insisted it was okay.

I just wished my body was how it was a year before.

At this point, we had my surgery scheduled for September 16th. That was almost exactly two months away, which felt like too far away but too close at the same time. I was antsy to have my scoliosis corrected, because I was hoping my left arm would return to normal. But I was also extremely nervous. My back and neck were going to be cut open, and I could die or become paralyzed again. If the surgeon even slightly touched my spinal cord with a tool, it could be a done deal. The terrible thought made me shiver.

My mom got a phone call from Dr. Sponseller's office when we were at home. "They can do your surgery earlier," she told me. "Do you want to do it earlier?"

"Yes!" I told her eagerly. "Please move it earlier!" I knew I needed to have it done as soon as possible if I wanted to save my left arm, so it needed to be as early as possible. When I took a second to think about what I'd just agreed to, my mixed emotions of anxiety and excitement came back. I was scared, because there were so many risks, but I was excited to hopefully feel better again and regain some of the independence I'd lost. But it really did hit me then: I was going to have surgery sooner than I'd originally thought. Sixteen days sooner. My surgery ended up getting rescheduled for August 30th. I wanted to have it done as soon as possible, because I was sick of being in pain 24/7, and I had a small ounce of hope within me that surgery could save my left arm. I was thankful my school went through grades 7-12, because I only attended four days of Freshman year before I flew to Baltimore for my pre-op on the 24th and surgery on the 30th, and it would've been even more difficult to miss school if I was a new student. My counselor helped me get friends lined up to take notes and send them to me, and my teachers sent me work I could do when I returned home.

At my pre-op appointment, my X-ray showed my scoliosis to be around 80 degrees. "I look like a dinosaur," I told my mom with a chuckle, trying to ease our anxieties. She laughed and agreed, and I was glad our close, silly relationship was still the same despite the severity of the situation. We both knew how to have a good laugh even while we experienced the worst.

Dr. Sponseller came to the conclusion that my left arm lost function most likely due to a stretch injury. Since my neck was curved so far to the right, all the muscles and nerves on the left side were too long, while the ones on the right were too short. This made it so the muscles and nerves on the left side of my neck had too far of a distance to travel to reach my left arm, which ultimately caused it to lose function. The pain and tightness I was experiencing were results of that, too. He reasoned that, since the surgery would correct my scoliosis and hopefully make my neck almost completely straight, the stretch injury would go away and I would regain the little bit of movement I had in my left arm. He couldn't guarantee anything, but we could all hope.

My spine would be fused from C4 to L1, which was quite a large portion. The rods placed during the surgery to straighten my spine would also help me hold my neck up. This way, my neck muscles wouldn't get as tired, and I most likely wouldn't be in as much pain as before. He told us he was going to decide the morning of surgery if he was going to go in from the front of my neck as well as the back since my curve was so high, which frightened me quite a bit. I didn't really want a scar on the front of my body, and I thought it seemed dangerous to go in from the front.

But I told myself I had to trust him. I picked him for a reason.

• • • •

Sarah Todd

    The night before surgery, my dad flew up to Baltimore. We all went out to dinner at my favorite restaurant in the inner harbor so I could have one last great meal before eating became difficult. I ordered my usual crab cakes, but I could only stomach eating a few bites. I hadn't really been *that* nervous until then. I'd actually been more worried about the blood draw for my pre-op than the actual surgery! Of course, I'd thought about all the things that could go wrong during the surgery, but it being the night before made everything feel too real. I had trouble getting to sleep that night, but it didn't really matter since I was going to be asleep for the entire day, really, starting at around 7:30 in the morning. We got up at 5:00 and drove to the Johns Hopkins Hospital Children's Center, where we checked in and waited. It might've been because I was so tired, but I realized my nerves were going away, and I was actually more excited, because I was hopefully going to be pain-free and regain my arm function! Jen even set an alarm so she could text me before surgery, which made me feel cared about and happy. My mom took a picture of me in the waiting room so we could see how my neck looked right before surgery, and my neck was so far to the right and my right shoulder was so much higher than my left that the One Direction boys on my t-shirt were standing slanted!

    When I saw Dr. Sponseller, he asked me how I was feeling, and I told him I was excited. I was *so* ready to not be in pain anymore. My words made him smile. "I'm glad we'll be able to do this for you," he told me genuinely. I could tell when a doctor truly cared, and he definitely did. He educated a few residents in my pre-op room before I got my IV put in, which was interesting to watch (especially when he had to correct them on things!). One of the residents put my blanket back over my legs as they were leaving and said, "See you later!" I had a feeling she meant she'd see *me*, but I wouldn't see *her*. Meaning, she'd see me on the operating table. That creeped me out a bit.

The nurse couldn't get my IV in. (Of course.) I'm known for being a bit sassy to doctors and nurses when they can't do their jobs correctly, so when the nurse couldn't get my IV in, I got super annoyed. IVs don't hurt if they're put in correctly and only require one attempt, but it starts to get really old when the nurse can't do it. My OR nurse eventually stepped in and tried to put the IV in for the second try, and I'd started to cry because I was anxious they weren't going to get it to work.

"I'm so sorry!" the first nurse said. "Is there anything I can do to make it better?"

She was nice, but I was annoyed. Nurses put in IVs all the time—how hard could it be for them? "Get it in on the first try," I quipped, making my parents laugh. What can I say? I was a fourteen-year-old girl about to undergo a surgery my surgeon declared was more painful than open heart surgery. I think they could cut me some slack!

Once the IV was finally in, the nurses wheeled me back to the OR. This was when I started getting really nervous. I asked a nurse to tell me some jokes to distract me, which helped a bit, but when I actually got inside the OR and heard the assistants moving the surgical tools around, I got even more anxious. It was weird hearing the clanking of the metal and knowing those same tools would be cutting me open in a matter of minutes. I tried not to think about it and instead focused on going to sleep. The nurse put the medicine in my IV, so I closed my eyes to make it work faster. I told my mom and dad that I loved them and asked them to tell my brothers I loved them, too. I just hoped I would be able to move when I woke up.

Up and Down

"There's just no telling how far I'll go"

- *Moana*, "How Far I'll Go"

Jen

Every year during the week after spring break, my high school had an event called "Writer's Week," in which various types of writers visited and presented onstage in the theatre during each period. And when I say that there were many different types of writers, I mean it: we got to see everything from novelists, to journalists, to slam poets, to songwriters. Being a writer, myself, this was always one of my favorite weeks of the year because I loved that these people with very clear passions for writing were also living proof that you can write for a living. I loved seeing so many of my classmates excited about certain presenters, too, and not just because they got to miss class for it. When a bunch of high schoolers swarm around to buy slam poetry books after watching a slam poet's presentation, form long lines to get a picture with one of the writers, and give up their lunch periods to see extra presentations or attend the writing workshops, you know you have an impactful event.

Before each guest writer came onstage, there was always a student presenter who read or performed a piece of their own writing first. I was frequently blown away by the talent of so many of my classmates, as well.

My friends often pestered me about sending in a piece of my writing to potentially be one of these student presenters. But as much as I loved writing, and as much as I loved being onstage for choir, I'd always been absolutely terrified of public speaking... Especially if I had to read my *own* writing aloud. I'd much rather sing even a solo in front of people than give a speech, oddly enough. And, anyway, my writing never seemed like anything special to me. My favorite writers, especially when it comes to poetry, paint with the most eloquent words, creating a picture interwoven with perfect details and rhythm. It's musical, even if there's no literal music, and I have never been able to figure out how to make my words do that.

Still, it *was* my senior year, and therefore my last ever Writer's Week and last chance to be a student presenter, so ultimately, I pushed past my fears of public speaking and insecurities about my writing and decided to give it a shot.

After lots and lots of searching through my existing written works, and plenty of brainstorming for new things I could write, I came to realize that it would probably be best to just choose my favorite thing I'd written. At the time, this happened to be a poem I'd written that past fall, which was all about the small, daily things you miss when you have a disability. The thought of reading such a poem out loud made me really nervous, as I knew reading something I'd written about my disability to a large room full of my classmates was likely to make me feel vulnerable, but I was pretty sure it would be the best choice.

....

In the days leading up to the day I was supposed to present my poem, I almost regretted this decision. A couple of my friends had been selected to be student presenters, as well, and I was so proud of them and their poems, but increasingly nervous about my own, which I was becoming less and less confident in as I heard everyone else's written works during the week. When my day came, I was prepared in that I was sufficiently rehearsed, but I didn't feel prepared in any other way.

"Um, hi," I said into the microphone after a teacher had introduced me. My voice wavered.

I glanced down at the first of four papers I'd laid out on the podium and began speaking, starting with the brief introduction I'd prepared.

"This poem is for a lot of people. When I wrote it, it was about myself and my friends, Alex and Sarah Todd," I started. "We all have a condition called Transverse Myelitis that altered our lives forever, and we've talked a lot about how it's weird that we miss the 'smaller' things more than we do the 'larger,' more obvious ones. After writing it and reading it over more, I realized that it could apply to a number of things. So this is for anyone with a disability, chronic illness, or even mental illness."

I then took a deep breath and began the actual poem.

"From the time I could hold a pencil,

Could form shaky letters with the graphite tip,

Only semi-legible,

I loved to write..."

Through my poem, I first told the audience about some of my favorite things that I loved doing before TM. I then went on to describe how it feels to no longer be able to do these things the same way.

Since I knew this poem almost by heart by now, I wasn't even really thinking about it as I read it. Before I knew it, I was on the last page.

"Because when so much of your life has been taken away,

When so much is missing,

You crave the little things

Day

After

Day."

As soon as the last word left my mouth, I rushed off-stage as quickly as I could, heading straight to where my friends were seated and paying little attention to the audience's applause.

The teacher who had introduced me came back out and introduced the guest writer who was presenting to us that day. We clapped as she came out and went right to the microphone.

"Before I begin, can we give another round of applause to the student writer who was just onstage? That was wonderful!"

Everyone clapped for me again, and I kind of wanted to hide.

But then the lady, a professional author, began talking about the things she loved about my poem. She liked the way I started it, and how it transitioned into talking about my disability and how it affects those everyday things. She'd been paying attention, clearly, and it was such a confidence booster to be praised for how I'd structured my poem and its content.

I no longer regretted the decision to do this, as it felt so nice to get the message of my poem out there to my peers, which I felt they could in some way relate to. Life isn't easy for anyone, and at times everyone needs to know that they're not alone.

It was surprising to find that the experience made me so much more confident in myself, in regards to both my writing and speaking. Public speaking still wasn't my favorite thing in the world, and I knew it was never going to be, but I now knew I *could* do it. That's honestly such an empowering feeling, because there are so many messages you can spread that way, and I now knew that I was capable of spreading them.

• • • •

When it's the spring of your senior year of high school, everyone begins counting down the days to graduation. My class was no exception; it's something we'd been looking forward to for so long, practically since high school *began*, so naturally, as the snow started melting and trees once again began growing leaves, we grew increasingly excited for what we knew was just right around the corner.

Since it came right after Spring Break, Writer's Week had been like turning-point, a sort of catalyst that seemed to accelerate the remainder of the semester. Suddenly, the "senior countdown" was starting, where each of the remaining twenty-six days of school had a certain theme corresponding to a letter of the alphabet. As I dressed up according to the theme for these days, I couldn't help but think back to watching the seniors do this my freshman year. Now, those seniors were *my* class. Very soon, it was prom—yet another thing I remembered watching the upperclassmen participate in when I was a freshman—then senior ditch day, and then AP exams.

As we got further and further into the alphabet, I realized so many "lasts" were occurring, and my excitement turned into a flurry of other emotions. I didn't think I was going to miss this place, but I was quickly realizing how ridiculous that initial expectation was; how could I not miss a place in which so much of my life had happened? Looking back on it, the past four years simultaneously felt like an eternity and the blink of an eye.

So much was going to change. That spring marked my last AP exams, last high school choir concert (with the choir director who had practically become family), last jazz choir rehearsal, last Best Buddies meeting with my buddy who I adored so much, last time going to school with all of my friends, last time opening the locker that had held my things for four years, last time buying curly fries from the cafeteria.

Jen

On the last day of school, as I sat in my eighth period class, I marveled at the fact that this was going to be the final time I'd ever sit in that classroom, or any classroom in that school. I still couldn't believe it; my brain fully expected to return there the next morning, or the next year, but I knew that wasn't going to happen. The next weekend, my name was going to be among the sea of names they'd call out during the 2016 graduation ceremony.

• • • •

I finally sat among the sea of green, around 300 graduates, filling the Field House on Graduation Day, clad in the cap and gown that had been sitting in my closet for months. A couple tassels hung off the side of my cap, and I fiddled with the light pink chords around my neck.

I'd just finished singing our "senior song" with the rest of the graduating choir students at the very beginning of the ceremony, and I was still a little emotional from that. After we'd finished the song, as we returned to our assigned seats, one-by-one we'd each given Mrs. White a big hug. I'd been in her choirs for the past four years, and I knew that was one of the biggest things I was going to miss.

Next, we all listened to a few speeches, including the valedictorian's. My eyes wandered to the bleachers to my right, where I spotted my mom—already ready with camera in hand—and the rest of my family. I noticed a bunch of my friends' families, too, all anxious for the moment when their kids would walk across that stage.

Finally, they began calling names. It went in alphabetical order based on last name, and since my last name begins with "S," I had a bit of a wait. However, people were going pretty quickly, and before I knew it, the end of the alphabet was approaching.

"Jennifer Starzec" was called, and I slowly walked across the small stage and grabbed my diploma. I smiled in the general direction of the photographer as he snapped my picture, and then I exited the stage, green diploma in hand.

Just like that, high school was over.

Final Forte

Up and Down

"Give me some morphine, is there any more to do?"

- Harry Styles, "Meet Me in the Hallway"

Sarah Todd

If I had known all that I was signing up for when I agreed to have surgery, I wouldn't have done it. But it's actually a good thing I didn't know, because the surgery really wasn't elective. The aftermath was awful to say the least. I miraculously didn't need a blood transfusion, but I still woke up in the ICU. I don't remember much from the first night except for meeting my nurses, everything looking blurry, and my anesthesiologist coming to check on me. But all those memories are extremely vague, each one feeling like it only lasted two seconds. My mom told me I woke up every few minutes and yelled, "Button!" because I wanted someone to push the button that gave me more pain medicine. I'm glad I don't remember how much pain I was in that night, because I do remember the pain I experienced a few days later, and it was excruciating. And I bet the pain the first night was the absolute worst.

The next day, I was moved to a regular room, where I stayed for the next six days. Spinal fusion surgery recovery is typically only about two to four days, but since several weak parts of my body were completely moved around, my recovery was going to take much longer. I don't remember this, either, but here's a funny story. Apparently my right arm was stuck moving up and down after surgery. Now, we look back on this moment and joke that I was at a Braves game, but it was really frightening for my parents at the time. (Not for me because I slept through basically everything!) My mom said she worried that I wasn't going to be able to use either of my arms then, which definitely would've been horrible. We knew of all these risks before going into surgery, but we did our best to believe they wouldn't actually happen. Luckily, an OT came in and gave me a brace to wear on my right arm, which kept it straight. The issue resolved within a couple days. Meanwhile, a PT came in and tried to get me out of bed. I was incredibly dizzy whenever I sat up, and it took three people to get me out of bed—just like in the beginning, in April 2010. The parallels to my TM onset disturbed my mom a lot, but the fact that this hospital stay was planned was reassuring. We *knew* I was going to get better, unlike six years before. Sitting in a chair was more difficult than I'd ever known. It reminded me of when my therapists made me sit at the piano during the church service at CHOA when I first got TM. My entire body hurt, and I couldn't hold myself up. Thankfully, the narcotics made me so tired that I usually fell asleep in the chair, so I didn't have to be miserable for too long.

Five days after surgery, I had to get in a wheelchair to get my post-op X-rays taken. Strangely, I don't remember much up to this day except a few details like odd dreams or hallucinations the narcotics I was on made me have. I remember I had this crazy dream that my mom and I were in my hospital room, when the ceiling sprinklers turned on and started spraying everywhere.

Only, they were spraying *lemonade*. I woke up dying of laughter, finding the dream hilarious in my weary state. The narcotics and anesthetic also made me *so* lazy, that I kept saying, "I want to tell you something, but I'm too lazy to say it," whenever I wanted to talk. This one made my parents laugh, because I actually used energy to tell them I was too lazy to talk. It didn't make any sense. My odd dreams, hallucinations, and sayings definitely kept us laughing. It's good to laugh about the sucky stuff in life rather than cry over it.

I couldn't stand to take my X-rays, so my parents had to hold on to each side of me. My spine looked *impeccably* straight, save for a small curve that had formed at the bottom that was there from the way I held my pelvis while standing. Regardless, the X-rays looked promising. We wouldn't know if the surgery actually worked to resolve my pain for a few more weeks, but it was nice to know that I was all straightened out.

My dad had to fly home shortly after the X-rays were taken, which made me feel teary. Whenever I have a tough medical experience, I always feel much closer to my parents. "I'm going to miss you holding my hand at night," I told him as we said goodbye.

On the sixth day, I walked around the floor with a PT. She only wanted me to walk one lap around the floor, but I didn't want to stop. "I can do another," I told her confidently and proceeded to walk around the entire floor again. My feet were wobbly, my head felt heavy, and I was kind of dizzy, but I did it. I was exhausted after that, so my mom took me around the hospital in the wheelchair. The statue of Jesus in the main dome of the hospital was always one of my favorite places to go (even though I've seen it about fifteen times now...), so we went there and explored. I noticed a lot of people were staring at me, but I didn't know if it was because of the wheelchair or the large dressing on my throat. It just surprised me that people would still stare even though we were in a *hospital*. But I just gave all of them my best smile like I always do. We passed some abstract paintings that were hanging on the wall near a little cafe, and I quickly told Mom, "Wait! Don't run over the little boy by the elevator!" Somehow, the narcotics had made me think we were by an elevator—*not* paintings—and that Mom was going to push the wheelchair right into a little boy. It was so weird how much the pills affected me. I was only taking half an Oxy at this point, too. I couldn't wait to get off those drugs.

Seven days after surgery, I was moved to inpatient rehab, which was connected to the hospital. The building was really old, so there were no private rooms. My roommate and I had to share a bathroom, but we each got a set of drawers and a chair for guests to ourselves. The chair pulled out into a bed, so my mom slept there, which admittedly was not the most comfortable place to sleep. It also took a lot of work to actually turn the chair into a bed, and every night, my mom had difficulty with it. "No one should have to work this hard to go to bed," she sighed as she tampered with the chair once again. I laughed, but she was right.

I had trouble sleeping there, too. The bed wasn't comfortable at all (especially after just having back surgery), so they brought in a soft cushion to put under my mattress. But that didn't help much, because my roommate kept turning the AC to 55 degrees! Mom bundled me up with sheets and blankets to keep me warm, but then I'd get too hot and take them off, making me go right back to cold again. The fluctuating temperature made it nearly impossible to sleep. And I had physical and occupational therapy for hours every day, so I really needed a good night's sleep. My roommate's snoring didn't help, either. Privacy is crucial when you're trying to recover, and I didn't have that. It really was not a restful place.

The good thing was I weaned off the narcotics pretty quickly, so I started only taking children's Tylenol. I was *so* sick of Tylenol by the time I'd gotten home; I was certain I drank at least ten bottles of the purple stuff. But the Tylenol was the main reason why I could leave inpatient rehab early: I wasn't taking narcotics anymore, so I really didn't need the 24/7 nursing care anymore, and I knew I'd sleep better in a hotel. I'd been in inpatient rehab for five nights, but my discharge date wasn't for two days. My grandparents had come to help out with my recovery, and they helped me "escape" from inpatient rehab… by packing up their van with all my stuff (even the balloons!) and getting me out of there! The nurses stared at me as I walked out of my room, but I tried not to look at them and held in my laughter.

"You know the kid is not coming back when the balloons are gone," my mom laughed. We *did* look pretty suspicious... we had suitcases and bags *and* my balloons with us, which basically screamed that we were leaving.

Things got even better when my granddad pulled the van up to the front of the building and the security guard exclaimed, "You guys getting to leave?!" My granddad replied, "Yep!" and the guard said, "Congratulations!" It was *hilarious*. I basically escaped from the hospital, and the security guard went along with it! Rumor got around, too, because when I went to Kennedy Krieger Institute (KKI) for outpatient therapy the next day, my PT said, "So, I heard you escaped the hospital in the middle of the night." I cracked up laughing. It seemed I was going to have a different reputation at KKI from now on!

My mom and I felt like we were in actual paradise once we arrived at the hotel. It was just the usual Marriott Courtyard we always stay in, but the employees there have gotten to know us, so they were excited to welcome us back. The bed (which I'd nicknamed Betty a few years earlier), felt like the most comfortable thing I'd ever slept in, and it felt amazing to wear normal clothes and not just pajamas. I started regaining even more independence in the hotel, too, because the more normal and less medical environment encouraged me to be more independent. I couldn't sit up on my own or look down at my phone, though, and whenever I tried using my phone in my bed, my vision got blurry. I got scared that my optic nerve had somehow gotten damaged or something (because I, of course, always think of those extremes), but the blurry vision wore off after a couple more weeks.

When it was almost time for me to return home after being in Baltimore for nearly a *month*, I decided to see what would happen if I lifted my left arm up. It had only been barely four weeks since my surgery, so I didn't know what to expect; I had no idea when—or if—I would get what little movement I once had in my arm back. It was easy to feel hopeless, not knowing whether or not I was going to be back to *my* normal. But to my surprise, I successfully lifted my left arm the tiniest bit, making me beam. "I moved my left arm!" I immediately told my mom. "It's really tired now, though." I quickly became bummed.

"That's amazing!" she exclaimed. "Remember, you're rebuilding muscle," she consoled.

It was weird having to relearn how to do literally everything again. Everything I did felt different than when I'd done it before because so many parts of my body were drastically repositioned. When I returned to school, I couldn't wear my backpack for the rest of the year, so I had to rely on my friends to carry my backpack to all my classes for me. It was difficult losing some of my independence, because I couldn't walk to my classes on my own, but I knew I'd be able to wear my backpack again next year. I hadn't realized how much I relied on my neck to sit up or how close my neck was to my right arm. Since my neck was now perfectly in the middle and straight, my right hand had to travel farther to reach my mouth, so feeding myself was much more difficult than before. I could no longer reach my face to put on makeup or wash it, either, which I was able to do very well before. So, I compromised, and I started putting my right elbow on flat surfaces and then bringing my hand up to my face so I could reach it. I'd always believed that I didn't truly have any drastic limitations—I just had to get creative—and that creativity was coming out more than ever now. And I'm fortunate enough to have all of the movement I had in my left arm before surgery back, too! My left arm gradually regained function as I worked in outpatient therapy at KKI, and a few months later, I was incredibly lucky to have my "normal" arm function back.

"All you gotta do is just believe you can be who you want to be"

- *Dear Evan Hansen*, "Sincerely, Me"

Jen

The summer after graduation flew by. Immediately after school ended, I went to Colorado with my family to visit my great aunt and uncle, and then, just a few weeks later, I flew down to Atlanta to visit Sarah Todd again. The summer was also full of all my friends' graduation parties.

All of that was very fun, but it went by too quickly.

After that, though, came a lot of college planning... And stressing. I had to pack my whole room and prepare myself for so many goodbyes. They were obviously only temporary "goodbyes," but still, I'd never been so far away from my friends and family for so long.

I was going to Truman State University in Kirksville, Missouri, which is about an eight-hour drive away from home. As nervous as I was for that, I was also excited for the new experiences and to begin working towards my degree.

I arrived in Kirksville with two cars filled with my parents, my youngest three siblings, and most of my possessions on Freshman move-in day in late-August, which was a whole week before all of the returning students would move in.

Up and Down

All of the accessible dorm rooms on campus there were large, single rooms with connecting bathrooms, and I was assigned one of those, which was pretty nice. My family helped me move everything in and set up my room the way I wanted it, but too soon, we had to go our separate ways, as they had to start their long drive home, and I had to begin my first mandatory event of the whole "Freshman Week" ahead of me.

Freshman Week was basically a way for us new students to get to know the campus. It was a relatively small campus with few buildings, and the majority of the buildings were pretty close together and centralized. Still, though, for me those first few days, it looked like a maze.

Luckily, by the time that week ended and classes began, I was way more used to the campus and was starting to feel more comfortable finding things. I couldn't wait to start learning things in my classes and for this college experience to begin.

• • • •

Naturally, I wanted to check out all of the extracurricular activities that this school had to offer. I knew I wouldn't be able to do every extracurricular that piqued my interest, but I attended informational meetings for a few that I could choose from.

I was already doing chorus at that school, which I was excited for, but I also wanted to see if there was anything swimming-related that I could do.

When I saw that they had a Swim Club, I knew that was just what I was looking for.

Swim Club met twice a week, and it was pretty casual, with swimmers ranging from really advanced to beginners. I was relieved by that, because I knew I wouldn't have to worry about standing out too much by being slower than everyone else or anything; the range in levels had to mean a range in speeds and everything, too.

Every practice, the girls who led the club would write a warm-up and workout on the dry erase board in the back. The lanes were divided up based on ability, and I ended up hanging out with the beginners. I was never able to finish the entirety of their workouts, but that was fine; I did as much as I could doing the strokes the way GLASA taught me, and it was the perfect way to continue my relatively new hobby in college. Though I'd always envisioned being on my University's cross country team, this was an okay way for it to turn out.

Up and Down

"I am brave, I am bruised, I am who I'm meant to be, this is me"

- *The Greatest Showman*, "This is Me"

Sarah Todd

I'd never really taken a shower on my own before. When I was eight, I was just starting to become independent. I'd just started to take showers when I was around seven, but my mom still stayed in the room to supervise in case I needed her. She was always scared I'd fall or something, understandably, but this made it so I never had the independence of showering on my own.

Of course, after I got TM, I *really* couldn't shower on my own. When I first came home from the hospital, my mom helped me shower while I sat in a shower chair. This went on for about a year before my mom felt confident enough that I could stand while she helped me. It took me a couple more years to actually get enough strength back to be able to wash my body on my own, but once I did, I only needed help with washing my hair, drying off, and getting dressed. Just being able to wash my body offered me a lot more independence even though I still needed help with most of my routine.

After my spinal fusion surgery, I became more motivated to learn how to do things on my own. And showering was my top priority. It was really inconvenient not being able to shower when I wanted to if my mom wasn't available to help me, and I felt a bit more awkward as I got older requiring so much help from my mom when I knew my friends were doing a lot on their own. I wanted to be a true teenage girl and get ready on my own just like my friends did. Their independence was the only thing I was truly jealous of.

    I was on a mission to take a shower by myself, but I knew I'd need an accessible bathroom in order to do it. A regular shower simply wasn't going to be doable for me. So, my wonderful occupational therapist took a shower with me to determine what accommodations I'd need installed, and from there, she, Mom, and I redesigned my entire bathroom! We tore out everything that was in there and remodeled it so I could be as independent as possible. A shelf was put in my shower so I could put my right elbow on it to lean over and reach my head in order to wash my hair; automatic soap dispensers were put in the niche so I could put my hand under the nozzle to get body wash and shampoo; a rain shower head was installed so I could rinse the shampoo out of my hair easily; a touchpad was installed so I could turn the water on and off and adjust the temperature with the push of a few buttons. A tall counter was connected to my sink counter so I could put my right elbow on it in order to reach my face to do my makeup as well as put my elbow on it to take my shirt off and put it on, and a hairdryer on a stand was placed on the tall counter so I could dry my hair without holding the hair dryer. It took an agonizing five months for my bathroom to be redone, but the wait was more than worth it.

When I used my shower for the first time, I got pretty emotional. I'd *never* washed my hair by myself in my entire life. At fifteen, I took my first shower by myself, and I finally really understood what I'd been missing.

Life truly is wonderful when you can be independent.

My independence and growing up were much different than they would've been if I didn't have a disability. Since my mom helped me get ready for bed, she naturally pulled my covers over me and kissed me goodnight, even up until I was a teenager. I never really knew if this was "normal." Did my friends' moms kiss them goodnight still? Or was I the only one? My mom still prepared my food for me because I couldn't do it myself, which I knew was normal to some extent, like family dinners. But *every* meal I ate was made for me. I wondered if my friends made mac and cheese on the stove for themselves like I wished I could do or if their moms still helped them. I started feeling a little bit in the dark. The line between normal and abnormal wasn't clear to me because I needed help with so many things.

But being able to shower on my own was a tremendous step towards my independence. I was now able to shower whenever I wanted to instead of having to work out a time with my mom, and I could even do *more* than just shower. Since taking a shower is the beginning of most people's routines, I could now do the steps that follow, too. My tall counter allowed me to put my shirt on, so I could get dressed and ready on my own (as long as my clothing didn't have any buttons or zippers, because I still had trouble with those). For my bra, I had to clip it first and then step into it and pull it up before putting my arms through the straps to put it on, which takes *forever*, but I was letting my creativity show! Being able to take a shower on my own made it so I could do so much more than just shower, to the point where I came to realize that I really only would need help with putting my hair up and putting on certain shoes. And, because I could reach my face to do my makeup thanks to my tall counter, I started getting really into doing my makeup. I watched tons of YouTube videos on how to do makeup well, and now, people always tell me how good I am at it! I had Jen take a video of me using my shower and bathroom so I could share my adaptation ideas with other people with disabilities, because I wanted as many people as possible to experience the joy that is independence.

It really is astounding how having independence can make such a big difference. I'd turn on my music and blast it throughout my entire room while I took a shower and dried my hair, singing and dancing crazily. I hadn't ever been this happy to simply *take a shower*. I found myself looking forward to taking a shower instead of dreading it, because I had time to myself and I could dance and sing and just be a normal teenager. I finally knew what I'd been missing, and I was incredibly jealous that my friends had been doing this for the past seven years that I hadn't.

Sarah Todd

It's something most people do every day—

    Something nobody ever thinks about.

Washing, drying your hair every which way,

    You do those things without a hint of doubt.

Sometimes I ask—just how do others do things?

But then I gather up my thoughts and think.

There is so much good and worth the world brings,

    But only certain parts are scrawled in ink.

I never asked for these hard challenges

    So that is why I must overcome them.

With every step, I gain advantages.

Those ugly thoughts I have learned to condemn.

I give the music a big number ten—

Since I was happy to be fifteen then.

Written May 12, 2017 after taking one of my first showers.

Up and Down

"Look around at how lucky we are to be alive right now"

- *Hamilton*, "The Schuyler Sisters"

Jen

Though I'd loved musicals since I was a kid, my love for musical theatre began to grow a ton throughout high school. I was always too scared to actually try auditioning for anything (besides the handful of shows I'd been in as a little kid), instead just staying within my comfort zone of choir, but I made sure to see every single musical that my high school put on ever since my Freshman year—many of them more than once—and I even continued this trend after graduating. However, I'd never seen a professional show; that is, until the groundbreaking new musical, Hamilton, announced it was coming to Chicago.

The day that tickets were released, my two oldest brothers and I bought the first ones we were able to get our hands on, using money we'd saved up for it. We then anxiously awaited the day of our show, which happened to be early January, conveniently during my winter break when I was home from Truman.

As soon as the familiar first notes of the opening number rang through the theatre, I was overwhelmed with emotion. It's one thing to listen to the songs on the cast recording, but it's another thing entirely to feel the beat of it swelling through the room and watch all the various nuances of the musical happen live on-stage. The lighting, set design, costumes, choreography, orchestrations... all of that completely captivated me, and I studied every technical aspect closely, taking in everything that made live theatre such a work of art. I was at the edge of my seat the entire time, really appreciating and finding myself interested in all of the subtle differences in these actors' interpretations of their characters in comparison to the original Broadway cast on the cast recording. And, of course, I was in love with and found myself paying close attention to every aspect of the incredible singing coming from not just the many featured characters, but the ensemble, as well. The many beautiful harmonies in the background vocals were really noticeable and moving.

All of that really made Lin-Manuel Miranda's genius work—the story, the lyrics, all of the underlying themes—come alive.

When Karen Olivo, the actress playing Angelica began singing in the song, "Satisfied," my brother and I looked at each other at the exact same time and mouthed, "woah," before facing the stage again. The whole scene of that song was simply breathtaking onstage for all the technical aspects like lighting and set, and also, of course, Karen Olivo's acting and vocals.

The show was over much too soon, but I knew as I exited the theatre that I was going to do that again—not just Hamilton, but any musicals coming to Chicago that I was interested in. I needed to see *Les Miserables* (my all-time favorite musical), *School of Rock*, and lots of others. I knew my brothers agreed, too.

I was the happiest I'd been in as long as I could remember, which sounds like it'd be a massive overstatement, but that experience truly was that incredible and indescribable. It grew my love and passion for music, and it gave me a lot of new experiences to look forward to, since we now actually realized that we could save up to see future shows and have a great time.

Once again, I was reminded that there was an infinite number of things that could make me happy; I just had to keep finding them. Disabilities and chronic illnesses can take so much away from people, and I hated that, but that's never the end-all-be-all. Slowly but surely, I was continuously finding a multitude of meaningful things that made me feel so joyous and confident—music clearly being a big one—and for that, I was grateful.

Up and Down

"You are on fire, you can rise higher, up in the sky"

- *Mean Girls,* "I See Stars"

Sarah Todd

Every medical professional I'd met had always said I'd be able to drive. Imagining myself driving with the way my body is sounded pretty scary, but I knew there was a way I could do it. When I turned fifteen, my mom and I started investigating driving options for me, and I got my driving permit two months after my birthday, just in time for my driving appointment at the Shepherd Center here in Atlanta. Shepherd has a whole assistive technology department with a driving specialty, so I met with two of the guys who specialize in assistive driving technology. I had my vision and muscle strength tested, and then they drove me to a nearby neighborhood in a *massive* van they had that could accommodate all types of disabilities because of its size. I was *so* nervous to drive for the first time, especially in the gigantic van! They even had to put cushions under me just so I could see over the dashboard!

Having a disability and bringing up driving is always interesting. My friends either didn't think about it and just assumed I could drive like everyone else, or they just assumed I *couldn't* drive like everyone else. But I know that I can do anything I aspire to do; my disability does not impede me. All I needed to drive was some car adaptations, which Shepherd had for me. I first started driving with a joystick that moved the steering wheel, and I started using the pedals with my right foot like everyone else does. The joystick worked pretty well for me, but it did take a while for me to adjust to how easily it turned the steering wheel. For some reason, though, I couldn't find the pedals with my foot, so I tried driving with one foot on each pedal. That's not the best way to drive, but they had me try it since one foot wasn't working out for me. But, as I figured, I kept accidentally hitting the gas and the brake at the same time, so driving with both feet wasn't working out for me, either. The driving instructor guessed I had some proprioception issues, which was why I had trouble finding the pedals. I'd always thought I would be able to drive with my feet like everyone else since my legs work, so I was a little disappointed I had this issue, but it turned out alright.

When I drove for the first time, I only drove for about an hour so we could find out where exactly I was in terms of adaptations. But I went back to Shepherd over the summer of 2017, and I drove for four consecutive days for about five hours each day. Because I had so much trouble driving with my feet, instead of trying to use the pedals, I tried driving with a different type of joystick that controlled the steering wheel, gas, and brake. All I had to do was push forward for the gas and backward for the brake, and move it left or right to steer. It was so much easier to drive this way because I didn't have to worry about finding the pedals.

My confidence grew each day that I drove, and I eventually made it out of the neighborhood and onto the main road. I was so nervous when I did, because I kept thinking about how if I made one wrong move, I could be seriously hurt. I even made the mistake of directing my gaze at the oncoming traffic, which automatically made me direct the van that way. Worried, I quickly moved the joystick so the car moved back into my lane, my body heating up out of fear. I discovered that I drove better when I didn't think too much about what I was doing, so I tried to talk to my instructor as much as I could so I felt more relaxed. When I did, the slight movements of the joystick came much more naturally to me, and I drove much better.

Apparently, the neighborhood residents had been watching my progress throughout the week, and one woman even stopped to talk to us.

"Is she driving that big thing?!" she asked my instructor, shocked.

"Yep!" he replied proudly. "And only with a joystick that moves this much." He made the tiny motions of the joystick with his hand.

The woman opened her mouth in shock. "Go girl!" she called.

I smiled. I'd just successfully driven with one hand.

Up and Down

Jen

> *"The darkest skies will someday see the sun"*
>
> *- Next to Normal*, "Light"

Jen

It was late April of 2017, and during the past few months that spring, my muscle spasms, tightness, and tremors in my arms and hands had been gradually getting a bit worse. In the past, I rarely got spasms in my left hand; since I'd gotten TM, the majority of my spasms had been in my right arm and hand, especially my fingers. I got them in my legs at times, too, which had increased a bit since 2014 (causing me to begin having to take a daily muscle relaxer at that time), but they were rare in my left arm, besides the occasional "jump" of my fingers if they were tired or something.

But, this spring, they were beginning to get really annoying. My right fingers had started doing this frustrating thing where they'd get stuck in a fist for a few minutes before I could release it, and it was doing that a lot when I tried gripping things with that hand, which made it more difficult to use it. My left fingers also started shaking a lot more than usual when I straightened them out and stuff. That wasn't an uncommon occurrence when my hands were really tired, but now it was almost constant.

When I returned home for our short Easter break, my mom, who happened to be an Occupational Therapist (so she probably looked at my hands a little more often than the average parent), even remarked that my left hand seemed a little weaker than usual. It was spring, though, so the weather was changing rapidly, which seemed like a sufficient explanation.

But, just a couple weeks after returning to school, this all changed.

I was video chatting with a friend one night while eating dry cereal, as it was the closest food within reach in my dorm room, and I was hungry. An aching pain started growing through my left arm and then, all of a sudden, my left hand just fell. I couldn't move my hand at the wrist and my fingers felt weak and difficult to straighten out. I kept trying to pick up the little Cheerios that I was snacking on, but I couldn't get my fingers to move well enough to grip them, so I gave up and put the box away.

It gradually got better, though, and by the next morning, my hand felt normal again. I shrugged off the issue from the night before and promptly forgot about it as I went to class, going about my day as normal.

That afternoon, as I was doing homework, my left ring finger kept insisting on staying down tight against my palm. I kept trying to straighten it by forcibly straightening it against my desk, but each time, it just went right back down as soon as I stopped paying attention to it and let my hand "relax." The next day, my middle finger started to do the same, then my pinky, followed by my index finger and thumb. By that evening, all of my fingers were stuck in a tight fist, which at some points was so tight that my nails dug into the skin of my palms hard enough to leave deep marks. It fluctuated a bit from painfully tight (enough to leave those marks) to a little looser, which wasn't as uncomfortable, but no matter what, I couldn't get my fingers even close to straight. During the times when they were a little looser, I could straighten them enough to almost wrap them around a thin water bottle, but at other points, I couldn't even get my fingers to go around a pencil.

It seemed a lot like those spasms I'd experienced before where my fingers locked up for a couple minutes, so I wasn't worried at first. But, the difference was, this time it didn't go away, and because it was lasting so long and continuously getting worse, it was impacting my independence a lot. Ever since I got TM, my left hand had been my good hand; my right hand had enough function to be a "helper," but I couldn't do very much without the use of my left. It was getting more and more difficult to write or type, brush my teeth, wash my hair, get dressed.

During all of this, I'd been talking my mom a lot for advice on what to do, and finally, after another day had passed and it still wasn't any better, she encouraged me to go to the ER. I begrudgingly agreed and got a friend to drive me.

When I got there, I went up to the front desk to check in and explained what had been going on. She handed me some papers to fill out, then took out one of those hospital identification bracelets.

"Give me your good arm for this," she said, meaning my right arm since my left hand was the one I was there for. It was really odd to hear my right arm being called the "good" one, since it had clearly been the worse one since 2011.

Kirksville was such a small town that the ER was completely empty except for me and my friend, which was a big change from the packed Chicago ones I was more used to. We sat in the waiting room for just a few minutes before they called me over to the back to go into a room. My friend had to leave at that point, and then I was completely alone.

After spending a few hours at the ER while the attending talked with my mom and home doctors on the phone, he decided to admit me and start trying extra muscle relaxers and IV prednisone the next day. That night, my arm hurt so much from how tightly it was contracted that I got no sleep at all.

· · · ·

The next day, the neurologist met with me and wanted to do yet another spinal tap and MRI. This was going to be the third spinal tap in my life, and the millionth MRI.

They began with the spinal tap, which I was terrified for after my first two experiences, and I didn't get a ton of warning before they came into the room with the giant needle and stuff. This time, they injected a local anesthetic and gave me Ativan as a milder sedative before doing the procedure. The Ativan didn't seem to kick in until afterwards, but it actually wasn't bad at all; the local numbed it enough that I just felt a light pinch. As soon as it was over, I felt myself drifting off to sleep.

I had choppy dreams involving rocket ships blasting off in front of me, and suddenly, I woke up. Except, I was still in a rocket ship. I couldn't get out, though, because it was a really, really enclosed space. Also, it was making frighteningly loud hammering noises.

I was really confused and scared, so I yelled for someone to help. The hard bed I was lying on moved forward, and I was out of the "rocket ship" to see a few people staring down at me...

Oh. It was just an MRI. I hadn't remembered going in there since the medicine had made me fall asleep, and it had just been incredibly disorienting to wake up in the machine when it had begun to wear off.

The nurses brought me back to my room, deciding to finish the MRI later, and when we arrived I saw that my mom and aunt were there. They had driven down to Kirksville to see me, which was really nice, because I was no longer alone in that unfamiliar hospital.

After they wheeled me to the hospital bed, I began to stand to transfer back to the bed. They asked if I needed any help, but I told them I was fine, I could do it myself. I always stood to transfer. But, as soon as I tried to stand up, my legs gave out completely, causing me to fall onto the floor right next to the hospital bed. I grabbed the bed to support me and kept trying to get back up, but I literally couldn't bear any weight on my legs at all. Finally, I let the nurses and my mom help me get back onto the bed.

That night, adding to the pain in my left arm, my back and legs began hurting a lot. They ended up giving me a Lidocaine patch for my back and Fentanyl for all the pain in general, which I really didn't want, but I figured the doctors knew best.

I stayed at that hospital for about a week, as they wanted to try a whole course of steroids (and the extra muscle relaxers) before trying anything else. But, though it had gotten a little better, all my fingers remained contracted, so they decided to transfer me to a bigger hospital in the nearest city, which was the University Hospital in Columbia, Missouri. They transferred me by ambulance, and the ride was about an hour and a half long, which was a little annoying because the bed in the ambulance was incredibly uncomfortable. My back and thighs were still hurting so much, and that only exacerbated it.

Finally, we arrived, much to my relief, and my mom and aunt met me there not much later. They brought me straight up to a floor, which actually happened to technically be that hospital's cancer floor; I didn't have cancer, of course, but apparently it was the only floor with an available room. I immediately noticed that it was a really nice floor with huge single rooms, though.

We met with the neurologist team there, who had talked to the one at the Kirksville hospital. They wanted to try doing plasmapheresis to see if that would help, which it would if there were antibodies in my plasma causing this worsening of symptoms, and the doctor was pretty sure there was something systematic like that going on. Though plasmapheresis is a fairly common treatment for disorders like Transverse Myelitis, so I already knew what it was, I hadn't had it at onset.

Early the next morning, they put a weird central line in the side of my neck, which had three ports coming out of it: two for the plasmapheresis machine, and one just for regular things like blood draws. Like the child I was (despite actually being 19 years old), I joked that it made me look like I'd been abducted by aliens, who were doing alien experiments on me.

When it came time for my first round of plasmapheresis, they brought in a huge machine and a bunch of little bags of pale, yellowish donor plasma. They attached my neck line to a couple tubes on the machine, then connected one of the donor plasma bags and a bag of saline to it and turned it on. The way plasmapheresis works is, the machine removes your blood through one side of your central line, spins it around really quickly to separate your plasma from the rest of your blood, and then returns the rest of your blood into your body along with the donor plasma and saline (fluids). Your old plasma ends up in a big bag on the top of the machine.

The whole session lasted about an hour, and I had to do five sessions over the course of ten days (so one every other day). During the second session, I suddenly began feeling really lightheaded and dizzy, so the lady operating the machine took my blood pressure. It had dropped pretty low and kept dropping, so she quickly pushed the buttons on the side of my bed to make my head go down and feet elevated. She then paused the procedure for a little bit and had the nurses bring me an extra bolus of fluids, which seemed to do the trick. During the rest of the sessions, she slowed it down, added extra fluids, and checked my BP regularly to make sure it didn't drop that much again. I did continue to have a little trouble with low blood pressure on those days, but luckily, those precautions helped a lot.

I also needed a copper transfusion at some point that week, as my copper levels were low, as well as a cryoprecipitate transfusion for low fibrinogen. It felt like there was a *lot* going on at once, and I just wanted it to be over so I could go home.

• • • •

There was a really nice, outdoor garden area at the hospital, and since the weather was getting really nice during my time there, my mom wanted to bring me out to it lot.

The first time I went out was *exhausting*. Sitting up in the wheelchair hurt my thighs and back, and I got fatigued very quickly. I enjoyed the warm, fresh air a lot, but I wasn't able to last sitting up for very long the first time. As soon as we got back to the room, I lay down and took a long nap right away. I didn't really know where that exhaustion was coming from, exactly—maybe from low blood pressure—but I felt pretty miserable and it was annoying.

Everything gradually improved from there, though. PT and OT came daily to get me moving, and my legs were back to my baseline (able to use forearm crutches and walk short distances) after a few days, and the back and thigh pain was gone around then, too. My arm no longer hurt, either, as it had become considerably more relaxed—I still couldn't quite straighten my pinky, ring, and middle fingers, but my index finger and thumb were pretty much back to normal. By the time I was discharged from the hospital, I had begun adapting to this level of function pretty well, and I was grateful that my left hand was once again my "good" hand, even if it was less good than before.

Up and Down

"Just stop your crying, it'll be alright"

- Harry Styles, "Sign of the Times"

Sarah Todd

I started off Summer 2017 the most perfect way: flying to Chicago to see my best friend! Both my parents came with me, and we picked Jen up from the train station, then took her to our hotel. I hadn't been to Chicago in three years, and I hadn't seen Jen in a year, so I was very excited. Our hotel was attached to Water Tower Place Mall, so Jen and I explored tons of fun shops and great restaurants there. I felt like our friendship dynamic was changing a little, but for the better; we were fifteen and nineteen, having known each other for five years already, and we were both getting more mature. Our sister-like bond was stronger than ever. I truly did consider Jen my big sister. It was fun being able to help each other do things, too: I could hold doors for her with my back or push the "door-open" button on the elevator, while she could help me carry and open things. I also was always there to glare at anyone who made snide remarks or stared at her.

"Look, she's in a wheelchair!" a girl around the age of thirteen said to her dad very non-discreetly in the mall food court. Her dad promptly looked towards me and Jen, so I promptly directed a harsh glare their way. We made eye contact, prompting the pair to walk away from us quickly. What was so interesting about a girl who uses a wheelchair having dinner with her friend? People don't say, "Look, she's walking!" when they see an able-bodied person out and about. And what was the difference? I was proud to be there to defend my best friend. There really was nobody else I'd rather spend my time with, and I loved how well we got along.

Jen is the only person who I want to film my dances, too, so while I was in Chicago, she recorded my dance I'd choreographed to Harry's new single, "Sign of the Times." I dedicated the dance to Harry and choreographed it to share my story of battling mental illness and how Harry helped me see the light at the end of the tunnel. My costumes represented different stages of my mental health, and the locations did, too: when I was inside (in the dark), I was sad, and when I was outside (in the light), I was happy. I start the dance in a black dress (black to represent sadness) sitting on a window sill with the curtains closed to represent the darkness of mental health issues. When I go outside, I'm wearing a bright colored outfit with a bomber jacket that looked a lot like one Harry had, which represents happiness and the *reason* for my happiness: Harry. And, at the very end of the dance, I return to the window sill and open the curtains, letting the brightness—my happiness—into the darkness. The message of the dance was very important to me, so I tried to make it as powerful as possible. I wanted people to know how kind Harry Styles truly is, and I wanted the conversation on mental health to improve. Filming dances with Jen had kind of become another thing we always did together, and filming such a powerful dance in her city was definitely amazing.

Things like filming my dances together remind me just how close Jen and I truly are. I wouldn't want anyone else filming my dances, doing my hair and makeup for them, or coaching me along. And I definitely wouldn't want anyone else as my co-author and big sister.

It was weird to think about how I wouldn't know Jen if it weren't for Transverse Myelitis. What we would both consider the biggest evil in our lives brought us together. We'd made so many memories together helping each other through our battles, and we understood each other like true sisters. I've learned that there are always positive things that come out of negative things, and our friendship is one of them.

I really do have so much to be grateful for.

Up and Down

"When I'm with you, I'm standing with an army"

- Ellie Goulding, "Army"

Jen

The last time Sarah Todd had come to Chicago was the time she surprised me in 2014— almost three years ago. Now, she was coming again, except this time, I knew about it ahead of time. I was so excited to see her again and for everything we had planned to do! It had been almost a year since I'd last seen her, so naturally, we'd spent a lot of time planning what we were going to do while she was here. We wanted to make the most of our weekend together.

"How about this one?" Sarah Todd asked, pointing to a pale pink top on the rack nearest to her. We were at an H&M in the city, trying to find a suitable top for our photoshoot that afternoon, which Sarah Todd's mom had so graciously planned for us. The photoshoot was going to be by a company called Flytographer, who were going to take pictures of us in the city.

The weather definitely could have been better, as it was cold and very windy, but still, we couldn't wait!

I went over to the top Sarah Todd was pointing at, grabbing it off the rack.

"It's perfect! It'll even coordinate with you, since your shorts are the same color!" I responded, already making the decision to buy it.

By now, though, we were cutting it pretty close to the time the photographer was supposed to meet us. We rushed back to the hotel, where we quickly touched up our hair and makeup before leaving to meet our photographer, Danielle, in the lobby.

Danielle began the session by chatting with us for a little bit, no doubt trying to get a sense of our friendship and what kinds of things we wanted to see in our pictures. Then, we began the shoot, first starting out by the pool in the hotel, but then moving on outside to places throughout the city. Danielle encouraged us to just talk and laugh and goof off as if we were just strolling the city alone.

"Let me sit on your lap!" Sarah Todd said at one point, giggling. I let her, then moved the joystick on my chair to go down the sidewalk. Every time a passerby looked at us oddly, or the chair hit a bump and caused us to lurch forward, we broke out in a fit of giggles.

Meanwhile, Danielle was capturing the entire thing with her camera, resulting in some of the most adorable photos ever.

Initially, I'd wanted to hide my wheelchair in those pictures by either standing or sitting elsewhere for each one. This device that I'd first viewed as a means of more independence back when I'd first gotten it in 2015 had grown to become such a pain, I'd lost that original view and instead began to only see it as a nuisance and symbol of "difference." But, though it hadn't made it into every single one of the pictures that day, it had made it into a lot of them, and instead of being "in the way" in those photos, it was utilized in a way that really helped show me and the dynamic of Sarah Todd's and my friendship.

I couldn't thank Sarah Todd or Danielle enough for giving me a little bit of confidence back.

· · · ·

"Do you remember when we took those ridiculous pictures at Uno's?" I asked Sarah Todd during dinner one night, reminiscing about the first time we met, all the way back in 2012 in Baltimore. She nodded.

"Yeah! You know, that booth over there," she pointed at the empty table behind her, "reminds me so much of the one we were sitting at in those pictures."

I looked over at the booth in question, and sure enough, it did remind me of the one at Uno's. I mean, most restaurant booths *do* look alike, and we weren't exactly eating at an Uno's again, but all that reminiscing had made it stand out.

That sparked an idea.

"We should go over there and try to recreate those pictures! Just for the fun of it," I proposed. Sarah Todd excitedly agreed.

We'd already finished eating, and the place was pretty empty. We left our own table and slid into the nearby booth.

"We were *so* little!" Sarah Todd exclaimed as we looked through our Uno's pictures on my phone.

"I know, right?" I agreed. "I can't believe we were only fourteen and ten there."

Now it was 2017, we were nineteen and fifteen, and our friendship was stronger than ever. At the time of those pictures in 2012, we had no idea what was to come: that our friendship would grow and last forever, or any of the ups or downs that life would throw at us.

"The past cannot be changed.

The future is yet in your power."

- Unknown

Up and Down

Afterword

Throughout any journey, there will always be ups and downs. We have realized during these many years since we were first diagnosed with Transverse Myelitis that the story doesn't end there. It doesn't end after the initial recovery, or years later, or ever. Our lives may have been changed forever because of our disabilities, but they're *our* lives, which we feel constantly resemble a roller coaster ride: full of rises and falls.

We have grown and learned so much from these ups and downs, which has culminated in motivating us to help others and bring about change. Our voices are being heard on several platforms as we advocate for what we believe in.

This entire series has taken us six and a half years to complete, and we now have three wonderful books as a result! We began writing about our journeys in 2012, when we were 10 and 14 years old; we are now at the end of our series in 2018, at ages 17 and 21. So much has changed in the past six years, including our writing styles, but our overarching goal for writing has remained the same.

This book may mark the end of this series, but it is certainly not the end of our stories! We will always continue writing, whether that be on blogs, social media, or elsewhere, and the rollercoaster that is our lives will keep going. It is still our hope to continue to use our writing to spread awareness, encouragement, and positivity.

Up and Down

Finale

Sarah Todd

My parents and I always thought my presentation of Transverse Myelitis didn't match up with the other patients we knew. Mom and I used to always say that I have a rare disorder, but I'm rare *within* that rare disorder. We'd basically determined that I most likely did not have TM, but that was my diagnosis on paper, so we just said I did. In 2014, cases of what doctors termed a "mysterious Polio-like illness" and later called Acute Flaccid Myelitis (AFM) came up in Colorado, and the presentation looked exactly like me. After doing tons of research and listening to podcasts about AFM done by Dr. Greenberg, Mom and I were sure I had AFM and not TM.

AFM is a subset of TM, meaning the disorders are related. While both disorders are very similar, they are also very different. TM is an autoimmune disorder that occurs when the body attacks the spinal cord, while AFM is not an autoimmune disorder and occurs when a virus that is not polio but similar to polio (researchers think one such virus may be enterovirus D68, i.e. a cold or respiratory virus or the virus that causes hand, foot, and mouth disease) attacks the spinal cord. AFM results in paralysis that is flaccid rather than spastic paralysis caused by TM. The grey matter and anterior horn cells are damaged as a result of AFM, while the myelin sheath is damaged as a result of TM. It also seems that TM generally results in chest or hips-down paralysis, while AFM results in either neck-down paralysis or paralysis of one limb.

When I became paralyzed from the neck-down in 2010, I was diagnosed with Transverse Myelitis because Acute Flaccid Myelitis was not known. But there had been clear differences between my case and most TM cases. Only my anterior spinal cord was affected (rather than both the anterior and posterior, i.e. typical TM), which explains why I only lost sensation for around 24 hours (sensation is on the posterior cord, so the inflammation from my anterior cord seeped through to the posterior temporarily). My paralysis is also flaccid rather than spastic, as my arms dangle and flop around instead of tightening up. I was also a quadriplegic and had an odd recovery pattern (regaining leg movement but not arm movement), and most TM patients I was surrounded by were in wheelchairs.

AFM appears in the news frequently when "spikes" of it occur what seems to be every two years in the fall (because illnesses go around that time of year). But much of the information given in the news reports is watered down. AFM is not as rare as it seems to be, but a full recovery is rare. Recovery patterns differ with each case. And washing your hands will not prevent you from getting AFM; it could prevent you from getting sick, but that is not guaranteed. If you get a cold, that does not mean you're going to get AFM.

In January 2018, I had an appointment with Dr. Greenberg in Dallas to determine if I had TM or AFM. Partly why I wanted to know which disorder I had is because vaccines are not a concern with AFM since AFM is not autoimmune, but I also wanted to prove those who thought AFM appeared out of nowhere in 2014 wrong. There was no official name for AFM until 2014, but that didn't mean that no one had it before then. And my mom and I were right: according to Dr. Greenberg, AFM expert, I had AFM and not TM. The news was truly groundbreaking. I was one of the earliest cases of AFM.

• • • •

This year, I've gotten involved with a fabulous organization called the Runway of Dreams Foundation, which strives to achieve mainstream adaptive clothing for people with disabilities and include them in the fashion industry. Getting dressed has been one of my main struggles when trying to achieve independence with a disability. I'm unable to do buttons or zippers, so finding clothing options that worked for me has always been nearly impossible. I always had to wear jeans and shorts without buttons and zippers or have my mom help me unfasten and fasten them. While shopping, I've said, "I love this, but it has buttons," too many times to count. People with disabilities are the largest minority group, yet there are hardly any doable clothing options available. But thanks to Runway of Dreams, Tommy Hilfiger recently released an adaptive clothing line with magnets instead of buttons and zippers, and I've been able to get dressed more easily with these clothes. I'm proud to be involved with such a wonderful organization that is making history for the disabled community.

For more information: www.runwayofdreams.org

• • • •

I've been so fortunate to have accomplished so much in the past year. Several magazines and publications have featured me and my story, and I've gotten to do charity work and attend some wonderful events. I never thought I would have the opportunity to be interviewed by *Seventeen* Magazine at their headquarters in NYC, have a double-page spread in *J-14* Magazine, or be recognized by dancer Nia Sioux and the Rockettes. Even Niall Horan from One Direction was so excited to receive a copy of *Determination* and reunite with me four years after I met him on my Make-A-Wish trip. He remembered me and congratulated me on publishing my second book. I've successfully raised so much awareness and helped spread my message of positivity to others who are struggling, and I have to say I'm very proud of that.

• • • •

Jen

After my first year of college at Truman, I decided to stay home for a year and finish up my general education classes at the community college while I figured out what exactly I wanted to do next. I was trying to decide between two future careers: Physician Assistant, or something related to English and writing, such as an editor. I really loved the idea of working in the medical field because I really wanted to make a difference in people's lives, much like how all of my doctors, nurses, etc. had helped me so much ever since I was thirteen. At the same time, though, I loved words, grammar, and writing.

I ended up settling on going into Speech Pathology, because I feel that would almost be like a sort of combination of both of those passions; I'd still get to help people and make a difference, and I'd be somewhat in the medical field, but I'd also be focusing on words and language. So, I am now attending the University of Wisconsin - Whitewater, which has a very good "Communication Sciences and Disorders" program, and getting that bachelor's degree there will be the first step before eventually getting my master's degree in Speech Pathology. So far, I am loving the school and this program, and it's nice to be only a little over an hour away from home!

• • • •

My hand and legs are still about the same as they were at the end of this book—I can walk short distances and use forearm crutches, but I still need a wheelchair for long distances. The two episodes of worse symptoms in 2014 and 2017 are thought to be exasperations of my original spinal cord injury brought on by something systematic, bringing on a sort of bad flare-up that never improved completely.

· · · ·

Last year, during the 2017-2018 school year, I got to do a lot of great things with my hobbies, which was fun. I took voice lessons at the community college and sang solos at two recitals (one at the end of each semester). It was a great way to continue to be involved with music and considerably improve both my voice and confidence.

I also began swimming with GLASA again, and this time, I actually competed! It was really cool to compete in a sport again, and the swim meets actually reminded me a lot of cross country meets, in some way. I ended up qualifying for and then attending the National Junior Disability Championships (NJDC) for swim in Fort Wayne, Indiana in July 2018. I had a great time there and definitely hope to continue swimming.

Acknowledgments

At such young ages, it is incredibly rewarding to be able to say we have written three books. It is so important to us to spread our message of positivity and encouragement to others who are dealing with life-altering challenges, which we hope our books fulfill.

We always wanted the *5k, Ballet* series to be a trilogy, and we are so proud to have accomplished our goal! We'd like to thank all of our friends, family, and everyone else who has supported us throughout the writing process. To everyone who has read our books and been changed by our journeys: thank you. You are who motivates us to keep writing.

Thank you to everyone who has taken an interest in our stories and featured us in different publications: Joey, Hannah, Toni, Lisa, Sandy and Chitra, Flytographer, Nia, and the Rockettes. You've helped us get our stories out there and reach our goal of spreading awareness and hope to everyone who needs it.

Each of us thanks the other for her support throughout this entire journey. We would have never finished this book without each other! Writing a trilogy together has helped us make so many unforgettable memories, which we will cherish forever.

About the Authors

Sarah Todd Hammer is 17 years old and a junior in high school. She has lived with Transverse Myelitis/Acute Flaccid Myelitis for over half her life now. She lives in Atlanta, Georgia with her mom, dad, and two older brothers. In addition to being a writer, Sarah Todd is a speaker, activist, philanthropist, and dancer/choreographer. Her dances can be viewed on her YouTube channel. Sarah Todd aspires to become a neurologist or psychiatrist.

Continue to follow her story on her website:
www.sarahtoddhammer.com

Jennifer Starzec is 21 years old and in her junior year of college. She has had Transverse Myelitis for seven years. Jen lives in Illinois with her mom, dad, four younger brothers, and younger sister. She is currently attending the University of Wisconsin - Whitewater, where she is working towards becoming a Speech-Language Pathologist.

Continue following her story on her blog:
www.jensjournals.com

Be Sure to Keep Up with the Girls

Facebook:

5k, Ballet, and a Spinal Cord Injury

Instagram:

@5kballet @sarahtoddhammer @jenstarzec

Twitter:

@5kballet

Website:

www.5kballet.com

Made in the USA
Columbia, SC
05 January 2019